Department of Social Security
Research Report No. 27

Ma... or Di... s

Alan Hedges and Andrew Thomas

with Jill Keegan and Wendy Duldig

London: HMSO

First published 1994

ISBN 0 11 762162 5

Views expressed in this report are not necessarily those of the Department or of any other government department.

A full list of other publications in this series is shown on page 84.

Contents

		Page
	Acknowledgements	iv
	Introduction	v
Chapter 1	Overview	1
Chapter 2	Strategic Issues	4
	2.1 Simplifying the disability benefits system	4
	2.2 'Whole person' assessment	5
	2.3 Triggers and signposts	6
Chapter 3	Making a Claim: Problems and Solutions	7
	3.1 Awareness and entitlement	7
	3.2 Reluctance to make a claim	10
	3.3 Dealing with the benefit system	11
Chapter 4	Carers	19
	4.1 Awareness and understanding of the benefits available	19
	4.2 The Carer leaflet – FB31	19
	4.3 Identifying with the label 'carer'	20
Chapter 5	Providing Information and Advice	21
	5.1 Awareness and sources of information	21
	5.2 Methods of disseminating information – views and experiences	22
	5.3 Providing information and advice – ways forward	28
Chapter 6	Advice Agencies	32
	6.1 The role of advice agencies	32
	6.2 Providing 'signposts' to disability benefit advice	33
	6.2 Agencies' information needs	33
Appendix	A Profile of Respondents	43
Appendix	B Further Methodological Details	47
Appendix	C Fieldwork Documents	51

Acknowledgements

We would like to thank all those people who took part in this research study for their time and willingness to discuss their experiences in such detail and with such frankness. Our thanks also to Richenda Ward and Dan Murphy for their help and advice throughout the study, and the staff at the local benefit offices who trawled their files as part of our sampling process.

Introduction

Background

People with disabilities form one of the major groups of recipients of social security benefits. The benefits available to them are numerous, and include: non-contributory benefits, such as Mobility Allowance, Attendance Allowance (both were replaced and extended by Disability Living Allowance in April 1992) and Severe Disablement Allowance; National Insurance benefits, such as Invalidity Benefit and Industrial Injuries Disablement Benefit; and Income Support, an income-related benefit, which can carry a special premium for people with disabilities. Carers may also be eligible for benefit through the Invalid Care Allowance.

Against a background of change – the creation of the Benefits Agency (BA), and the introduction of the Disability Living Allowance (DLA) and the Disability Working Allowance (DWA) in April 1992 – the Department of Social Security (DSS) is concerned to ensure that the benefit information and advice services it offers should meet the needs of this significant claimant group.

The basis of this study has, therefore, been to explore people's experiences and attitudes towards the process of claiming disability benefits. A qualitative, rather than quantitative, research approach has been used to investigate possible difficulties with the benefit claim process and the factors influencing the take-up of disability benefits.

Social and Community Planning Research (SCPR) were commissioned by the DSS to undertake an exploratory study.

The aims of the study

The central aim of the study was:

- to identify the benefit advice and information services that would best serve the needs of people with long-term sickness or disability.

Subsidiary aims included the identification of:

- the problems that people with disabilities, or carers, have in gaining access to benefit information;
- gaps in people's information requirements that need to be overcome;
- the information needs of formal and informal advisors;
- the types and formats of benefit information that are required; and
- making recommendations that could enhance the delivery and dissemination of disability benefit information.

Research design, coverage and method

The research was designed to cover a range of different benefit types, and to collect information from people with a wide range of disabilities and benefit claim histories. Claimants included people with mental health problems, learning difficulties, and problems of mobility, sight, hearing and communication. The majority were in receipt of at least one disability benefit; some had been turned down for one or more benefits (unsuccessful claims). Both informal and formal carers were interviewed, as well as representatives from statutory and voluntary agencies that provide benefit advice or information to people with disabilities, at either local or national level.

Because of the strategic nature of the study, the programme of work was carried out in two stages. The first stage was concerned with identifying information needs, views and responses to existing benefit systems, and potential solutions to problems arising. This information was used to inform and focus the second stage of the research. This involved looking at how people's information needs could best be met – identifying ways of disseminating information, considering alternative presentation methods, formats and media, and suggesting potential solutions to the special problems that people with disabilities may face in making a claim for benefit.

Current recipients, claimants with failed claims, and informal carers were selected for interview from a pool of names obtained through local benefit offices. The research involved a combination of depth interviews (69), paired interviews (10) – usually a claimant and their carer – and group discussions (17). In total 153 people took part in the study (claimants – 68; carers – 43; representatives of organisations providing benefit and disability-related information and advice – 42). Fieldwork was carried out during the periods August–November 1991 (Stage 1) and May–July 1992 (Stage 2).

The study was designed with a wide coverage, both in terms of the diversity of respondents, as well as a wide range of issues. We have therefore tended to pursue broad themes rather than issues in detail.

Topic guides were used by the interviewers to provide a framework for the conduct of each interview, or group discussion, although the coverage of issues was largely determined by the participants' views and experiences. Stage 2 considered a variety of different materials for improving access – computer routines, tapes, literature, and so on. These were used primarily as stimulus materials, considering the concept rather than the detail. Consequently, it was not the intention of the study to conduct thorough tests of particular documents, formats or media. Depth interviews and discussion sessions lasted an average 1¼–1½ hours. They were tape recorded and transcribed verbatim. A detailed analysis of the transcripts forms the basis of this report.

Further methodological details and a profile of respondents are shown in the Appendices.

The report

The results are described in six chapters. The first comprises an overview of the problems experienced by people with disabilities in accessing the benefits system. Chapters 2 and 3 consider the range of problems experienced, together with some suggested solutions – Chapter 2 considers these at a strategic level; Chapter 3 considers changes that might be made to the benefit system as it is presently structured. Chapter 4 continues by considering the information needs of carers; Chapter 5 with the ways in which the dissemination of benefit information and advice might be enhanced. Chapter 6 discusses the information needs of benefits advisors (both formal and informal).

Many of the recommendations of this report have resource implications. The research team fully recognises that resources are tightly constrained, and that this in turn will have implications for the report's findings. Nevertheless, it was not felt appropriate for these constraints to be superimposed on the study evidence – the report should be seen as an agenda of issues that need to be raised when considering the design and implementation of benefit-related services for people with disabilities.

Notation used in this report

The following notation is used throughout this report:

AA	Attendance Allowance
BA	Benefits Agency
BAP	Benefit Advice Package
BEL	Benefit Enquiry Line for people with disabilities
CAB	Citizens' Advice Bureau
DIAL	Disablement Information and Advice Line
DLA	Disability Living Allowance
DSS	Department of Social Security
DWA	Disability Working Allowance
HB	Housing Benefit
ICA	Invalid Care Allowance
IIDB	Industrial Injuries Disablement Benefit
IS	Income Support
IVB	Invalidity Benefit
LBO	local benefit office
LOAF	Local Office Administration File
Mob A	Mobility Allowance
NI	National Insurance
SCPR	Social and Community Planning Research
SDA	Severe Disablement Allowance

Throughout the report we refer to current benefit recipients, as well as people who have received a disability benefit in the past, or have failed in their claim for benefit, as 'benefit claimants'.

It is notable that claimants are generally unaware of the creation of the Benefits Agency and continue to refer to the 'DSS', or even the 'DHSS'. For this reason we use the general term DSS/BA throughout the report.

Chapter 1 Overview

Views about, and experiences of, the benefits system were many and varied. For some people, the process of making a claim for benefit worked quite satisfactorily in its entirety; they appeared to be in receipt of their full entitlement, the processing of their claim had progressed without obvious fuss, and they felt very satisfied. Others, however, were not so satisfied and expressed disenchantment with one or more aspects of the claim process. Yet others did not appear to be claiming additional benefits despite the prima facie case for entitlement.[1]

People with disabilities experience problems with the benefit system at two distinct levels:

1. They experience **the same problems as other benefit claimants**, which may include:

- lack of knowledge of the benefits available;
- lack of understanding, or misunderstanding, of the benefit system;
- lack of awareness of the existence of leaflets and/or difficulties in finding the appropriate leaflets;
- problems with understanding forms and leaflets;
- the size of forms (described as '*daunting*');
- uncertainty about benefit entitlement;
- a reluctance to claim benefits because of:
  - a sense of shame or guilt about receiving State benefits;
  - fear that they may not be entitled to (additional) benefits;
  - fear of being rejected;
- lack of confidence about coping with the benefit system;
- a dislike of Benefits Agency offices because of:
  - lack of privacy;
  - long waiting times;
  - unpleasant image;
  - an unwillingness to be associated with claimants who are long-term unemployed;
- perceived inefficiencies in the social security system due to:
  - delays;
  - lost papers;

1. The research team were not in the position of making a full assessment for benefits; we cannot, therefore, be sure about a person's entitlement, although the evidence was often strong.

- errors;
- misinformation;

- mistrust of the social security system because:
  - '*they don't want to pay out*';
  - '*they're not there to help*';
  - '*they don't tell you what you're entitled to*';
- not knowing what questions to ask (and assuming they need to know) in order to claim their full entitlement;
- difficulties with understanding the interrelationships between benefits;
- not being given reasons for/not understanding why benefit claims have failed;
- lack of awareness and understanding about re-assessment, review and appeal procedures.

These are the main problems, and sometimes the only problems, that people with disabilities report about the benefit system. Improving access to the benefits system in general would also improve access for people with disabilities as well.

2. In some instances additional problems with the benefits system arise **because a person has a disability**. This may be for a number of reasons:

- there are more benefits to know about and make a claim for;
- the interrelationship between overlapping benefits is even more complex;
- some issues specific to people with disabilities, such as the need for medical assessment;
- a benefit system that has been primarily designed for people who are not disabled and therefore poses problems where a person has:
  - impaired sight, e.g. reading leaflets and forms;
  - impaired hearing, e.g. finding someone in local benefit offices with whom they can communicate;
  - speech difficulties, e.g. as above;
  - mobility impairments, e.g. getting to the local benefit office and/or medical examination;
  - limited dexterity, e.g. completing forms;
- dependence on others to find out about their benefit entitlement and to make a claim.

The report makes many recommendations for action to tackle the above problems. These arise purely from the research, and we have not tested their practicality, cost, or policy implications.

In the **short-to-medium**-term some of the most important steps seem to be:

- identifying and promoting (and perhaps resourcing) local centres of expertise and advice in disability benefits, both in the voluntary sector and within the BA **(Section 6.2, Recommendation 19)**;
- providing health and social services professionals with simple 'signposting' materials which enable them to refer clients to these local centres **(Section 5.3, Recommendation 16)**;

- providing a new range of literature which advises people how to deal with the disability benefit system, rather than trying to explain its intricacies **(Section 5.3, Recommendation 17)**;
- initiating better triggers to activate secondary claims or re-claims, and better 'signposting' between benefits **(Section 2.3, Recommendation 3)**;
- giving staff more training in disability issues, and developing named disability specialists in each local office **(Section 3.3, Recommendation 9)**;
- developing, promoting and re-branding the Benefits Enquiry Line (BEL) **(Section 5.2, Recommendation 15)**;
- initiating better triggers to activate secondary claims or re-claims, and better 'signposting' between benefits **(Section 2.3, Recommendation 3)**;
- developing audio and video tapes as user-friendly media for disability benefits information **(Section 5.2, Recommendation 14)**;
- improving the distribution, display and appeal of literature **(Section 5.2, Recommendation 13)**;
- finding better ways of collectively addressing people with disabilities **(Section 3.1, Recommendation 4)**;
- developing simplified literature to help claimants who have reading difficulties, which would enable them to take more control of their financial affairs **(Section 5.2, Recommendation 13)**;
- sorting out problems with the new medical self-assessment forms (including the definition of 'needing help') **(Section 3.3, Recommendation 7)**;
- rationalising and reducing the collection of duplicate information through claim forms **(Section 3.3, Recommendation 6)**;
- publicising and clarifying the disability benefits that are available to carers and claimants with disabilities, and to encourage take-up **(Sections 3.1 and 4.1, Recommendations 4 and 18)**;
- improving decision letters to clarify the reason for failed claims and suggest subsequent action **(Section 3.3, Recommendation 11)**;
- improving payment options for some benefits **(Section 3.3, Recommendation 12)**;
- providing clearer information about the benefits that people are actually receiving **(Section 3.3, Recommendation 12)**;
- encouraging co-operation and partnership between DSS/BA and the voluntary sector **(Section 6.1, Recommendation 19)**;
- discontinuing, or remodelling the existing technical leaflets, and reviewing the provision of information and materials to advice agencies **(Section 6.3, Recommendation 20)**;
- reviewing the need to promote benefit assessment computer packages for advice agencies **(Section 6.3, Recommendation 20)**.

In the **longer term** many of the problems currently experienced would be ameliorated if:

- the structure of the disability benefit system was considerably simplified – fewer disability benefits with clearer names **(Section 2.1, Recommendation 1)**;
- the disability benefit system moved towards 'whole person' assessment, in which a single claim triggers assessment for all relevant benefits **(Section 2.2, Recommendation 2)**.

Chapter 2 Strategic Issues

2.1 Simplifying the disability benefits system

Problems with accessing the disability benefits system are exacerbated by the fact that a person with a disability is potentially eligible for a number of different benefits, the names of many of which are said to be confusing and sometimes misleading. For example:

- There are felt to be too many benefits, which have to be separately claimed. It is not obvious to claimants why the number of benefits could not be rationalised and simplified. For example, one benefit for people with disabilities and one for carers, with special provisions, or supplements, to take account of different needs and circumstances. This, it was felt, would be easier to learn about, understand, and claim.

  '... the benefit system is so complicated. So if you take that complicatedness away from an individual they don't have to worry about the ins and outs of filling in forms, or their National Insurance contributions ... of being told you can have this and not that ... make the whole thing simpler to understand ... and to get in to.' (Advisor)

- Benefit names do not necessarily give commonsense, or intuitive clues to their nature. For example, the main difference between SDA and IVB is whether a person has paid sufficient NI contributions, although it is not apparent from the benefit name. Similarly, some people who are eligible for SDA do not consider themselves to be 'severely disabled' and raise the point that there is no apparent reason why people who qualify for SDA should be considered more severely disabled than those entitled to IVB. AA and ICA are also commonly confused, with some people considering AA to be a carer's allowance.

- Some benefits refer to 'disability' or 'disablement', others to 'invalidity'. While this may be due to historical accident, there does not appear to be any obvious relationship between the name and the nature or purpose of the benefits. In addition, while some people felt that they could identify better with the terms 'disability' and 'disablement', 'invalidity' was felt to be both old-fashioned and stigmatising (see Section 3.1). The distinction between 'benefits' (as in IVB) and 'allowances' (as in SDA) was also rarely apparent to claimants.

- The interrelationship and overlaps between different benefits is seen as an additional obstacle to understanding the benefit system and allowing ease of access – advisors, in particular, pointed out that the way in which various combinations of benefits interacted with Income Support made understanding the disability benefits system exceptionally complicated.

These features, concerning the way the benefits system works, never seem to be explained to people, and sometimes causes misunderstanding and friction. For example, the benefits system is structured on the assumption that the onus is on claimants to make a claim for any benefits they think they might be entitled to – but this feature is not made explicit in the literature – and some people make the incorrect assumption that the system will provide them with their complete entitlement. Respondents questioned whether this is the way the benefits system *should* work – but as long as it does then the fact should be made clear to people.

However, there was considerable enthusiasm for the simplification of both the structure of benefits and their names. While it is clear that *any* change in the benefits system tends to cause problems and confusion in the short-to-medium-term – and respondents are already irritated by the rapidity of change in the benefit system – nonetheless, there seems to be strong 'customer' feeling that in the long-term, the system of disability benefits needs radical change.

RECOMMENDATION 1

a. Simplify the structure of disability benefits by:

- reducing and amalgamating the number of different benefits;

- using more meaningful, memorable and intuitive names.

b. Clarify benefit overlaps and interactions.

2.2 'Whole person' assessment

There is an underlying assumption on the part of claimants that the way in which the social security system *should* work is that LBO's should inform a potential claimant of their **complete benefit entitlement**. However, one of the most common criticisms of the social security system is that '*they don't tell us what we're entitled to*'.

We mentioned in the previous section that the benefits system is seen as too complex, by virtue of the number of benefits, and the way in which they inter-relate. However, the complexity of the benefit system would matter far less if the approach to benefit take-up considered the claimant as a whole. The opacity of the benefit system would be irrelevant to the majority of claimants, provided there was a 'front end' which allowed ease of access.

At present, this suggestion is the diametric opposite to the way in which claimants see the social security system – that is, unless a claimant knows their precise entitlement, they are unlikely to receive all the benefits to which they are due. This suggests a strong case for a 'whole person' assessment, which if it could be credibly implemented would dissolve many of the existing problems with access to benefits. The idea is that rather than making separate claims for specific benefits, people would make a general series of statements about their circumstances, and would then be assessed for any benefits to which they might be entitled. Theoretically this might apply with advantage to all benefits, but in the present context we consider this in relation to disability benefits. The snags and problems are obvious (the risk of even longer forms, for example), but the advantages seem very considerable.

> *'If it was a system where you could get in touch with the DSS and give your financial circumstances once, and they can then come back and say, "You are actually eligible for this, this, this and this. You are not eligible for this, this and this because..." you are then in a situation when you can either take up and make your claim for those .... You can appeal as to why you're not eligible for the others, but you've only done that once.'* (Advisor)

> *'... the sensible thing would be to have a unified section within the DSS which deals with all benefits for people with disabilities and for people with ill health. And I think at the moment there are three, four, five ... the lack of scope for effectively advising a person as an individual when you've got five different sections seems to be magnified.'* (Advisor)

RECOMMENDATION 2

Explore the possibilities of 'whole person' assessment, triggered by a single claim.

2.3 Triggers and signposts

Simplifying the system of disability benefits should be a major long-term goal. In the interim there are various other possible steps that can be taken. So long as people are required to claim each benefit separately, there should be better *signposting between benefits* in order that people who claim one benefit can be alerted to other relevant benefits that they should consider claiming.

There should also be thought given to claim 'trigger' points. These might be:

- **Conceptual triggers** – helping customers to learn to recognise circumstances which should trigger a fresh claim. For example, people might learn that they should claim (or re-claim) a certain benefit if their condition deteriorates.

- **Procedural triggers** – procedural triggers could be engineered into the system itself, which would either automatically trigger a claim, or a re-claim, in a given set of circumstances, or flag the advisability of making such a claim. A good example of this might occur with IIDB. At present, with the industrial injuries claim procedure, claimants can be advised to make a claim for benefit after a specified period of time has elapsed – occupational deafness claims are typical of this. The onus, however, is on the claimant to pursue the claim; a procedural trigger built into the IIDB system should be able to initiate re-claims automatically in cases such as this.

- **Change of circumstance triggers** – changes of circumstance tend to be a problem with benefit administration. Two situations affecting people with disabilities were mentioned:

  – when people move in and out of hospital or residential care; the system is sometimes said to be slow to adjust;

  – conditions (such as MS) which can be highly variable, to the extent that people may need periods on and off benefits. Some say, in these cases, that the claim is cancelled during lengthy periods of remission, and then a fresh claim has to be made. The need for a more flexible approach to handling claims of this nature – a claim which would remain active, but only provide benefit as needed – was called for.

Claimants tend to see their relationship with the DSS/BA as adversarial in nature – the job of the DSS/BA is seen as being '*to show why people are not entitled to benefit*'. Amongst the study respondents there was considerable support for having a designated person within the social security system whose job is to maximise a claimant's benefits within the regulations, to look for additional benefit entitlement, and to argue the claimants' cases. Respondents felt that the 'designated person' should be a member of the front-line staff, such as a counter clerk, where they would be in day-to-day contact with claimants. While there is evidence to suggest that this does happen to a very limited extent, and on an ad hoc basis, the overall impression is that this is neither the aim, nor the practice, of the DSS/BA. There was considerable support for a reversal of this perceived position.

RECOMMENDATION 3

a. Greater signposting between related benefits.

b. Develop both **procedural** and **conceptual** triggers to claiming.

c. Develop better ways of dealing with short-term change.

d. Consider developing claimant advocacy within the social security system.

Chapter 3 Making a Claim: Problems and Solutions

In this chapter we consider the disability benefit system as it stands at present, and discuss the types of problem that people with disabilities have in making, and pursuing, a claim for benefit, together with a number of suggested solutions.

3.1 Awareness and entitlement

Respondents often had only the vaguest knowledge about the disability benefit system. A number of features were evident:

- lack of awareness of the range of disability benefits available;
- poor understanding of entitlement to disability benefits;
- poor awareness of the benefits they were receiving. For example, respondents used the expression, '*I get the disability benefit*,' which was variously used to refer to SDA, IVB, AA, MobA and DLA;
- an assumption that the DSS/BA would be paying them their *full* benefit entitlement.

Ignorance of possible entitlement sometimes continued for many years – dispelled belatedly in some cases (often by a chance event); in other cases still persisting at the time of interview. For example, there were respondents in the study who were found to be:

- unaware of ICA, even though they may having been caring for a relative for many years;
- unaware of the Carers' Premium (and of IS premiums in general);
- confused between AA and ICA in terms of eligibility;
- unaware of AA and MobA (now DLA) even though they had been physically disabled for some time.

This general lack of awareness of the disability benefits system appeared to be due to two major factors. First, some respondents simply do not come across the relevant information or literature that would enable them to decide whether they should make a claim for benefit. (We deal with the issue of information dissemination and distribution in detail in the next chapter.) Second, despite the literature that is available in public places, some respondents do not perceive the leaflets as being relevant to them – they do not identify with the way in which leaflets describe people with disabilities.

Addressing people with disabilities

A common theme throughout the interviews was that the disability benefit system is seen as applying primarily to people with physical and/or mobility impairments. While it is recognised that it is important not to stereotype people – claimants are all individuals and think of themselves as such – publicity and advertising materials inevitably address people in terms of groups. The primary disability information leaflet (FB28 'Sick or Disabled?') is an example of this, addressing the entire population of people with disabilities with the label, 'sick or disabled'. It is clear that all people with disabilities do not identify with this collective label, for a variety of reasons:

- There is a preference for emphasising a person's abilities, rather than their disabilities.

- People with disabilities have a very wide range of conditions and circumstances and do not necessarily feel kinship with everyone else who might be labelled in the same way. This was particularly evident for people with mental health problems, learning difficulties and communication problems. Similarly for people with gradual, variable or 'invisible' disabilities. Carers, too, had difficulties in recognising the person they cared for as 'sick or disabled', particularly where they were looking after a young child or an elderly relative.

- The terms 'sick' and 'disabled' tend to have very narrow meanings. For example, the term, 'sick', is associated with short-term illness, sickness and disease; 'disabled' is associated with physical disabilities, in general, and people in wheelchairs, in particular.

  ' "I am disabled," still has that wheelchair element. "I have a disability," can be literally anything.' (Claimant)

This has clear implications for the way in which benefit-related materials are designed. Overall, there was a substantial feeling that the current all-embracing 'Sick or Disabled' was inappropriate; respondents with very different disabling conditions expressed preferences for different ways of being addressed. For example;

- The term 'health problems' tend to be associated with relatively minor short-term illnesses.

- 'Invalid' and 'invalidity' were generally seen as referring to frailty; they were also felt to be old-fashioned and stigmatising terms.

  'Well, invalid conjures up a very old person with a zimmer frame to me .... I think certainly that if that was put on a form it would be a little off-putting. I don't like it; it doesn't really describe what's wrong with me.' (Claimant)

  'Invalidity – I don't like the word, because I think it can make one feel worse than one already does.'

- 'Mental health problems' was generally felt to be 'too global', preferences being expressed for more specific or colloquial terms such as 'depressed', 'anxious', '*suffering from nerves*', stress problems, or clinical labels such as 'agoraphobia'.

- 'Mental handicap' and 'learning disabilities' or 'learning difficulties' were used interchangeably, although parents were rather persistent in their use of 'mental handicap'. Views were mixed about the various terms. While 'mental handicap' was felt, in some cases, to be stigmatising, others felt that the use of the word 'learning' related to difficulties such as dyslexia, rather than more profound problems.

  'We had a meeting at my son's centre, and someone said that one of their local shopkeepers had said, "If you come and ask me to do something to help the mentally handicapped, I'll help them because I feel that they need help, but if you say, will I do something to help people with learning difficulties .... Well, I'm not really very interested; I can't see there's very much wrong with them." And so for trying to sort of say it nicely, and say my son has learning difficulties, they think, "Well, he just needs a little bit of help," whereas if you just come out and honestly say he's mentally handicapped, they say, "Right, he needs a bit of help," and they'll do something .... You do think, though, that it's [learning difficulties] just that they can't read or write .... Yes, they're just a bit slow.' (Carer)

- 'Blind' and 'visual impairment' were also used interchangeably. Views were mixed with some people feeling that the term, 'visual impairment', diminished the problems that they experienced.

Solutions are difficult to generate, and are complicated by claimants, carers and advisors having differing views about the suitability of different ways of addressing people with disabilities. So, while some carers were content to continue using terms such as 'mental handicap', and even 'backward', professionals tended to use terms such as 'learning difficulties'. In this context, claimants also use a wide range of terms, although often expressing disabilities they have in terms of reading, remembering or learning. It is, therefore, important to find more appropriate and effective ways of addressing the population of people with disabilities. The evidence suggests that there are two potential solutions which could be used together or in isolation.

First, although not as 'snappy' as the expression 'Sick or Disabled?', the following description (based on that shown in Appendix C, Show card F) was felt to be both generally acceptable, and applicable to people with a wide range of disabilities:

Do you have any kind of physical or mental condition which makes it hard (or impossible) for you to:

- get a job?
- look after yourself?
- get about?

Second, an alternative approach to the question of addressing people with disabilities (in terms of attracting their attention) is to address their particular disability (for example, multiple sclerosis, cerebral palsy, arthritis, etc.), although this would have very significant cost, distribution and display implications. 'Grouping' similar conditions together was felt to be a 'best-compromise' solution, targeting leaflets at specific groups of people with, for example, mobility impairments, visual impairments or mental health problems.

> *'I mean, she is not sick and she is not disabled as such, in a wheelchair. I don't think I would have taken a lot of notice because she does not fall into either of those categories. Could they have stuck "blind" on? You might have taken a bit of notice then, when it is your own problem. It would have caught my eye, because I never look for anything else knowing that she does not come under that.'* (Carer)

> *'If there was a book [leaflet] with "nervous problems", or "problems with nerves" it would be helpful.'* (Carer)

RECOMMENDATION 4

a. Consider publicity campaigns to:

- increase awareness that benefits exist for people with disabilities, and carers;
- increase awareness of the *specific* benefits available;
- increase broad understanding of entitlement, i.e. who the benefits are for;
- encourage people with 'invisible' disabilities and family carers to claim benefit.

b. Reconsider the methods by which people with disabilities as a whole should be targeted by:

- replacing the existing term 'Sick or Disabled?';

- considering the use of broader-based questions, such as:

  Do you have any kind of physical or mental condition which makes it hard (or impossible) for you to:

- get a job?
- look after yourself?
- get about?

  - considering the use of 'group' labels which have a narrower and more targeted approach such as people with 'mobility problems', 'visual impairments', 'mental health problems', etc.

3.2 Reluctance to make a claim

For some people there is a general reluctance to make a claim for benefit. This tends to be for three main reasons:

- **An avoidance of 'hassle'** – some people shy away from the 'hassle' they feel claiming involves. This includes having to fill in long and intrusive forms, having medical examinations, becoming 'tangled up' with official processes, and laying one's private life open to strangers. Combined with general feelings of stress, fatigue and diminishing independence, this may de-motivate some people from either making a first claim for benefit, or pursuing additional benefit claims. In some cases avoidance is based on past experience, in others it is as a result of the folklore and the '*they won't give you anything*' attitude that continues to persist.

  'DSS is a Big Brother image to the average person. It's the authority; they have enormous powers; it's an image created by them and, therefore, the average person is always a bit hesitant about getting involved. They don't want to do it wrong, they want to get it right.' (Claimant)

- **Losing their existing entitlement** – overlaps and interactions are a perceived difficulty for some claimants. In some instances claimants are puzzled and angry to find that the amount of a new benefit they have received has been deducted from their, or their partners, benefits. Others hesitate to make a claim for fear of jeopardising their existing entitlement.

- **Shame, guilt and fear of rejection** – in some cases feelings of embarrassment, shame or guilt about claiming benefits inhibits people from enquiring about, and making a claim for, benefits.

  'I think there's a stigma. When you do hear people gossiping, "Ooh, look at her, she's on the Social, she gets this, she gets that," and, "Look at her, all them kids, and I bet she's on the Social." I don't know if it's my upbringing, but I felt as if I was getting something I shouldn't have had. At first I were sent giros, weekly, and then I got a book, and I had to stand in line at the Post Office to get this money, and I used to think I should really be going to work; I shouldn't be getting this.' (Claimant)

Some respondents who were already in receipt of one benefit said that their reluctance to claim further benefits was 'guilt about being on benefits. I don't feel I should be claiming this [benefit] but I have to survive.'

'I've been in carers' group meetings, and we've discovered that there is somebody there who could be getting Attendance Allowance for the person they're looking after, and they could get Invalid Care Allowance. We go through it all and they decide, "No, I don't want to do it." Now, that's because of the kind of issues we started off talking about, the bureaucracy, the fact that there will be people coming round their house and prying into their lives; the

fact that as a carer she may feel that she's failing in some way. All those kind of broader issues about why they're not going to claim.' (Carer)

There were also some examples of respondents' unwillingness to make a claim for benefit because of a *'fear of rejection'*.

RECOMMENDATION 5

- **a.** Consider a take-up campaign designed to legitimise claiming disability benefits.
- **b.** Ensure better 'signposting' between benefits.
- **c.** Clarify benefit overlaps and interactions.
- **d.** Trigger cross-benefit applications, where possible.

3.3 Dealing with the benefit system

In this section we consider a number of features of the benefit system that were felt to need attention: benefit claim forms, medical examinations, communicating with the DSS/BA, hearing the decision and methods of benefit payment.

Benefit claim forms

Respondents have very mixed views about completing claim forms. For some people, forms have become a way of life, and they are untroubled by the requirement of form-filling. Others, however, felt that forms could be a major problem:

- having to provide large quantities of, often very personal, information; a feeling that is intensified by a sense of inquisition and of being tested;
- the length and complexity of the forms (particularly the new DLA/DWA forms), which could be a deterrent to making a claim;
- being unsure about what the form is asking, and worrying about inadvertently giving the wrong information;
- a feeling that much of the information required is not relevant or necessary;
- perceived repetition of information within, and between disability claim forms;
- a view that the DSS/BA has much of the information already from previous claims for benefit;
- having to complete separate forms for each benefit, particularly where there is perceived to be considerable overlap in terms of content;
- having to complete forms again, from time to time, either for trivial changes in circumstance, or to confirm that they still have a disability from which 'recovery' is impossible (such as spina bifida).

While the research team were not required to consider the introduction of the new benefits DLA/DWA in detail, a difficulty with the new forms was found to have arisen. A key issue that appears to need clarifying is the definition of 'needing' help, particularly where a person is *not receiving help*. Both advisors and claimants say that this is a major problem, partly because it dissuades some people from making a claim, and partly because some of those who do complete an application are felt to have seriously understated their need for care. The difficulty is that people seem to feel that:

- the benefit is specifically to pay for help, and by definition if a person does not currently receive help they are not entitled to the benefit or, conversely, if they receive the benefit they feel that they *must* spend it on buying in help; and

- that if a person does not have any help, they do not (by definition) 'need' any help – '*I manage,*' was a phrase repeatedly heard in this context.

  'People getting Attendance Allowance can spend it however they want. And if you read the form that's not very clear. When you're saying, "What help do you need?" it doesn't fit with people who perhaps are managing living by themselves. And it also gives the impression that if you get your £36 a week, or whatever, you're then going to have to buy in such and such kind of support, which isn't the case again.' (Carer)

RECOMMENDATION 6

a. Look for ways of shortening and simplifying benefit claim forms.

b. Clarify the definition of 'need' in the new DLA claim packs.

c. Reduce the length of claim forms by attempting to use the information DSS/BA already holds for a claimant.

d. Consider a single form for all disability-related benefits (length would be a problem, although some of the material would be duplicated).

e. Avoid asking people to make regular confirmations of stable medical conditions.

Medical assessment

Medical examinations form part of the claim process for almost all of the disability-related benefits. While some people were fairly happy with their experiences of medical examinations, a number of criticisms emerged:

- the need for medical examinations was questioned, with respondents querying why their own doctors' or specialists' medical examination was not accepted as evidence. There was some feeling that DSS/BA medical examinations were unnecessary duplications;
- the perceived inadequacy of medical examinations to cope with conditions that are variable, or which have periods of remission;
- brusque or insensitive treatment by medical practitioners;
- a lack of information and advice about the nature of the medical examination, the nature of the precise tests carried out, and their relation to the eligibility conditions of the particular benefit;
- the need for multiple medical examination when applying for more than one benefit – '*... couldn't they just do one [medical] examination to cover all the benefits I claimed for?*';
- often lengthy journeys, under stressful conditions, for what are seen as short, unfriendly and unrealistic medical examinations.

The problems that people experience in medical examinations is made all the worse by two factors: the feeling that medical examinations are carried out as a means of detecting fraud, and second, that some claimants try to portray their disabilities in the best light, thereby limiting the effectiveness of the medical examination. For example:

- Throughout the interviews there was a feeling that medical examinations '*may not be all they seem to be*'. The folklore plays its part – there is a view that if a person is able to get to the medical examination, this in itself is a trap as '*if you can get there you aren't that bad*'. Respondents who had experienced 'invisible' health problems or mental health problems felt in particular that they were suspected of being fraudulent in their claims.
- People with disabilities prefer to stress their abilities, rather than their disabilities. Some take care to present themselves in the best light as often as they can, including at medical examinations. They do this by resting for

the day before the medical examination and minimising the amount of help they might need – '*I manage*,' is the phrase used. The effect is to understate their difficulties which may have a deleterious effect on the outcome of their claim for benefit.

> *'It was very nerve-racking because you have a doctor come and give you a test. It's a horrible thing to have to do, actually, because you have your child in front of you, and you have to talk about how he can't do anything, which I think is horrible. You go through your life trying to pull your children up and support them and tell them how good they are in what they do, and there you have to sit for an hour, hour and a half, telling a complete stranger how useless they are, and it's horrible. It really is a horrible thing to have to go through.' (Carer)*

With the advent of DLA/DWA the traditional medical examination has now been complemented by self-assessment. Despite the problems associated with 'traditional' medical examinations, both the principle and the practice of self-assessment were of concern. Notably, self-assessment was seen:

- to shift the (often worrying) burden of the responsibility for certifying a person's disabilities from the medical profession to the claimant themselves. Respondents were worried about whether they would be able to answer the form 'correctly', and were concerned that if they did not do so they might prejudice their claim. Similarly, advisors were concerned that claimants might not be able to present their case sufficiently well, either because of difficulties in describing their problems, or by minimising their problems – '*I manage*';
- to make people with disabilities think about their *problems* rather than their *abilities*;

> *'People with disabilities find it quite a change in viewpoint, when for most of their lives they're trying to emphasise what they can do, the positive side of their lives, the strengths of themselves. Never mind the disability. And you have to sit down and fill out a 47-page form that actually emphasises all the things you can't do, or the help you need. I think that's difficult.'* (Claimant)

> *'When they've filled in this form they're making light of the problems because they don't like to admit. They've always tried to be positive. If they're saying that they can wash in the morning and actually all they can do is sort of flick a bit of water around – they don't really wash, but they like to think they can do it. It's very hard if they have to confront that and put it in writing ... page after page of saying, "My wife, husband or daughter does this for me," and they've finished the booklet and they think, "Oh, pass me the gun, I can't do anything."'* (Claimant)

- to add a large number of difficult and detailed questions to claim forms that are already seen as too long;
- to include questions that were ambiguous in their meaning and unclear in the way in which they should be answered – particularly the questions that refer to the 'need' for help (see Section 3.3).

RECOMMENDATION 7

a. Offer claimants the choice of medical examination or self-assessment.

b. Use medical examinations as sparingly as possible, particularly where a person is making simultaneous claims for different benefits.

c. Consider accepting evidence from GPs and hospital consultants.

d. Examinations should be as local as possible; where mobility is difficult home visits or transport should be provided.

e. The precise purpose of the examination and the individual test performed should be explained to claimants.

f. The results of medical examinations should be communicated, and their relationship to decisions about the claim explained.

g. Give further thought to self-assessment procedures, to:

- defuse the sense of responsibility/anxiety about giving 'wrong' answers;
- clarify why questions are asked;
- to give better definitions and explanations of 'needing' help.

Communicating with the DSS/BA

Respondents may have communicated with the DSS/BA in a number of ways – visits to the local benefit office, by telephone and letter. A number of issues arose in this context: worries about dealing with the DSS/BA; understanding who to get in touch with; dealing with BA staff; and getting to and using local benefit office facilities.

Worries about getting in touch with DSS/BA

Respondents expressed two main worries: a general apprehension about dealing with the DSS/BA;

> *'The last time that I were at the DSS I were very disillusioned with it, and I think, basically, I've been fortunate that I haven't had to go back. Had I had to go back it would have been under a tremendous amount of pressure, a tremendous amount of pressure. I'd have gone with someone to lean on. I'd have probably taken my mum, or my brother would have gone with me. If I'd had to go on my own I'd probably have laid there and starved to death.'* (Claimant)

and not knowing what to say to the DSS/BA staff;

> *'Have you ever rung them up? I let my mum 'cos I don't know what to talk about really. I don't get involved with 'em. I don't understand 'em myself, 'cos everything's changed so much and it's so complicated.'*

Knowing who to get in touch with

The distinction between centrally and locally administered benefits is not well understood by claimants. Claimants would prefer a single point of reference for all their benefits, wherever the benefit is administered – the administrative structure should be transparent to the user, although this does not currently seem to be the case.

Problems with finding out about centrally and locally administered benefits occurs either where the person makes an enquiry by personal visit or by telephone. The perceived potential cost of making long-distance telephone calls to find out about the progress of benefits is also inhibiting.

Additional issues arise when claimants do get in touch with DSS/BA. First, they felt that it was difficult to know whom to ask for, and second, where there are subsequent calls, there was said to be lack of continuity in dealing with the case. Case papers were also reported as 'missing' or 'out of the office'. From some claimants' perspectives the DSS/BA appears to be in certain ways disorganised and incompetent; claimants also become angered at 'being given the run-around' and worry about the cost of 'the ever-increasing phone calls'.

> *'"That's Blackpool," they said, "and nothing to do with them" ... sent the book back – and I had to wait another three months for that coming back then. And the address had changed at Blackpool, and I wondered if they'd lost the book, or something. I went back there [local office] and asked them but they still*

wouldn't help .... [They] give me Blackpool's number. Spent £2.50 and got nothing. She said, "Stay in the phone box, we'll call you back," but when I looked on the box it said it doesn't accept in-coming calls.' (Claimant)

'The problem is that the DSS itself is so split up. You have a local branch which does, say, Income Support, or whatever. And then you have records up in Newcastle; you've got Blackpool administering this ... split up all over the country.' (Claimant)

RECOMMENDATION 8

a. Consider making the central/local administration of benefits transparent to claimants.

b. Aim for a single point of reference, as far as possible.

c. Consider the need for continuity of staff in dealing with case-related enquiries.

Dealing with BA staff

Front-line local office staff are sometimes said to lack:

- general knowledge and expertise in the range of benefits available;
- specific expertise in benefits for people with disabilities;
- training to deal in a natural, sensitive and reassuring manner with people who have disabilities which may affect their ability to communicate and/or may make them embarrassed or sensitive.

'Because I'm disabled they assume that I'm mentally disabled; they treat me like a small child.' (Claimant)

To some extent this was felt to arise because the crucial (and often difficult) customer interface was often handled by the most junior and least trained members of staff. The high degree of compartmentalisation between different benefits was also felt to be implicated in DSS/BA's inability to provide an enquiry service that is comprehensive and has continuity.

'Well, there's no privacy. Everybody that's sitting around can hear you saying everything ... the way you're spoken to as if you don't understand anything. I mean it's the people that are sitting behind the counter that belittle people when they go in. I think it's extremely wrong.' (Claimant)

'A lot of the front-line staff who get involved with [disabled people] for the first time, in fact I think on the DSS's own admission, that they are not all that experienced, and that turnover of staff is very great.' (Claimant)

'Usually ringing the DSS for advice is not a terribly useful procedure because you don't get a helpful response and you don't get a very informed response.' (Claimant)

'The front-line advice tends to be at junior levels, and in terms of raising confidence and being more likely to get accurate advice, it's having higher grade, longer serving staff both doing the visits and the front-line advice on the desk, and that doesn't happen – and that's essential 'cos a lot of problems get missed.' (Claimant)

RECOMMENDATION 9

a. Consider having a named 'disability advisor' in each local office, specially trained in the range of disability benefits, and trained to provide a sensitive and reassuring service.

b. Move further towards using staff names and/or named case officers.

c. Consider the general level of training and benefit expertise of all staff, and in particular front-line staff.

d. Provide social skills training to local office staff, with particular reference to people who have learning difficulties, mental health problems and communication problems.

Local benefit offices

A wide range of views are held about visiting local benefit offices. In general, there is a feeling of distaste. To some extent this is due to respondents not wishing to identify with people who are long-term unemployed – the group of people who are perceived to be the primary users of local office facilities. There are also a range of additional reasons, some of which are based on experience, others on the 'folklore' that surrounds social security:

- long delays;
- lack of privacy for the discussion of personal and sensitive issues;
- a 'generally unpleasant environment';

> *'The DSS office in [area] in particular is on the first floor and there is no lift; you have to go up a flight of stairs before you actually come to a reception area where there are a couple of security guards and so on. Then there is one hall on the first floor, and then another one on the second floor; the lift is constantly used as a toilet because there aren't any toilets in the building, and the whole place is a dreadful place.'* (Claimant)

> *'There's this, probably well-founded, belief that most Benefit Agency reception offices are horrible, dark, dingy places … no loos … or probably on the second floor, so if you've got a wheelchair you can't actually get in there in the first place. There's this image that the Benefits Agency is, to its credit, trying to dispel, but it still sticks and there's quite a strong image in many people's minds.'* (Claimant)

For some people with mobility problems, difficulties with transport and access make the use of local benefit offices very difficult, if not impossible.

> *'They have a ramp to this new wonderful office but she can't get her wheelchair through the door. Now that is appalling.' (Carer)*

However, the problems with local offices that have already been discussed were said to be greater inhibitors of their use. If problems of delay, privacy and the general office environment were to continue, then phone enquiries or home visits were felt to be the most acceptable ways of dealing with benefit-related problems.

RECOMMENDATION 10

a. Continue to improve local benefit offices.

b. Review the availability of home visits.

c. Consider providing transport, where necessary.

d. Adopt better appointment systems for people with disabilities.

Hearing the decision

There is considerable feeling that the decision letters that are sent to claimants are very formal in tone, legalistic in nature (particularly for IIDB) and lack clarity.

Decision letters are also felt to provide little indication as to why claims might have failed, nor meaningful advice on what to do next where a claim has failed. A benefit refusal can sometimes be devastating – people may feel that they have been judged to have been trying to obtain a benefit for which they are not entitled. This can dissuade them from appealing, re-claiming later, or making a claim for other benefits they may be entitled to.

RECOMMENDATION 11

- **a.** Decision letters should be revised (across all benefits) and designed to be courteous, easy-to-understand and informative.
- **b.** Notifications of failed claims should be humanised and made less formal and discouraging.
- **c.** People should be given reasons for the failure of a claim. This should be related to their condition and any medical assessment. Conditions under which a re-claim might be successful should be suggested.
- **d.** 'What-to-do-next' information should be provided with all decision letters. These should indicate:.

  - conditions that would trigger a valid re-claim;
  - signposts to other benefits;
  - review and appeal rights (in *easy-to-understand* form);
  - advice on sources of expert help and advice.

Payment of benefits

Views about how benefits should be paid were mixed, with some preferring cash (by payment book), and others expressing a preference for credit transfer into bank or building society accounts. The key feature to emerge is that respondents would like to be offered a choice *for all the benefits they receive.*

It was not uncommon to find that claimants were hazy about the benefits they were receiving. While in part due to the number of benefits available and benefit names that are less than memorable (see Section 2.1), this is exacerbated by inadequate details of benefits on payment books – it was often difficult to identify precisely which benefits respondents were receiving, or how the amount was made up, from the details provided on payment books alone. Although claimants receive award notices setting out their benefit entitlement, these are not, in some cases, seen as adequate; they refer to a single benefit and do not give an 'overall picture' of a person's benefit entitlement, and they do not appear to be updated with changes in benefit rates. Greater detail on payment books and a regular 'benefit statement' was requested as this would provide claimants with a greater amount of up-to-date information.

The tendency for DSS/BA to refer to benefits received by the generic 'disability benefit' rather than the precise benefit name adds to the confusion that respondents experienced.

RECOMMENDATION 12

- **a.** All disability benefits should be paid either in cash (payment book), or by credit transfer to either a bank account, a building society account, or a Post Office account.
- **b.** Claimants should be able to choose the method of benefit payment for all benefits.
- **c.** Payment books and other documents should provide clearer and fuller information about:

  - which benefits are received (including IS premiums, higher and lower rates, etc.);
  - how much is paid under each benefit, and in total.

d. Claimants should receive periodic 'benefit statements' which list the benefits they receive, the amount of each benefit, and an explanation for any changes in amount.

e. DSS/BA should ensure that in *all* communications the precise name of the benefit is used, rather than the generic 'disability benefit'.

Chapter 4 Carers

4.1 Awareness and understanding of the benefits available

Carers are often under severe pressure – time and stress. Some are also unable to leave the person they are caring for except by arrangement, with a consequent restriction of their mobility. Against this backdrop, it is perhaps, not surprising to find that the information that informal carers have about the benefit system tends to be, at best, patchy, and at worst, incorrect.

Typically, carers have:

- little understanding of the distinction between benefits for which they are entitled to claim (e.g. ICA), and those benefits for which the person cared for is likely to be eligible (e.g. AA, now DLA) – considerable confusion still arises between ICA and AA;

- limited awareness of ICA per se, and poor understanding of the eligibility conditions.

In addition, some advisors also reported very limited public awareness of the IS carers' premium – a finding confirmed by carers themselves; some advisors also thought that the IS carers' premium had been missed off the Benefit Agency's IS computer.

> *'And the lady down the [benefit] office, at first she said, "Well, there's no such payment" [carer's premium]. And I said to her, "The Citizens Advice Bureau said there is." .... And she said, "Oh well, I'd better go and have a look in the books," and she came back afterwards and she said, "Yes, I'm terribly sorry, there is, so obviously we've been telling people there's no such payment and there is." So there's quite a lot of people probably that have been turned away for it.'* (Carer)

4.2 The carer leaflet – FB31

By the time of the Stage 2 fieldwork the new carer's leaflet (FB31) had been released, and should have been in circulation. At the time of the study very few carers or advisors were aware of, or had seen, the new leaflet.

While it was not our intention to test vigorously the new FB31 leaflet, and there was only limited time within the interviews to examine it, first impressions were generally fairly favourable. For example;

- some people felt that they learned new information that might be useful, even after a very quick inspection;

- the list of 'helpful organisations' at the back of the FB31 leaflet was often liked, with some people finding out about organisations that were directly relevant to them for the first time.

> *'Very good [of FB31], what I've seen of it so far. It's more interesting than the other things I've had before; better set out altogether.'* (Carer)

On the other hand, some criticised the leaflet for:

- poor quality paper and printing;
- an overly selective list of helpful organisations which, it was felt, did not sufficiently represent child-related organisations, and those that dealt with people with hearing difficulties;
- a cover design which drew mixed reactions, some feeling that it gave too limited a view of the range of 'caring relationships' that were likely to occur.

> *'Well, looking at the front of the leaflet it's caring for the very young or very old. I wouldn't have picked it up and thought it was anything to do with me.'* (Carer)
>
> *'I don't think I would [see it for me]. I'd have looked closer – it's a little Down's Syndrome girl isn't it? And I wouldn't have put myself in the same category as having to look after a little girl or an elderly person.'* (Carer)

4.3 Identifying with the label 'carer'

Although the term 'carer' was generally seen as acceptable and appropriate – a term with which people in the caring role generally identified – there was one group of carers for whom this was not the case. 'Family carers' – instances where the carer was from the same family as the claimant – tended to be problematic. While this mainly occurred where the carer was a parent, there were some instances where respondents were looking after spouses or elderly relatives. In these instances, there was a tendency to see the caring in which they were involved as a 'usual' family relationship – 'it is something a mother does; look after her child' – rather than as a special role. For some carers it, therefore, never occurred to them that they might be entitled to claim benefits as they were simply carrying out their 'usual' family role.

> *'I don't associate caring with what I'm doing with my child. I'm merely bringing up a child.'* (Carer)
>
> *'Carer to me means outsiders; someone who comes in to look after someone. "Carer" would be someone who comes in from the outside; it's not sort of a personal sort of word really.'* (Carer)
>
> *'I wouldn't give it [FB31 "Caring for Someone" leaflet] two minutes thought because the words "caring for somebody" there just means a foster home. It's looking after somebody else but not [in] a father and child relationship, or mother and child relationship.'* (Carer)

RECOMMENDATION 13

a. Clarify the names of benefits which carers can claim.

b. Publicise and promote ICA; encourage take-up.

c. Promote and encourage general disability benefit awareness amongst informal carers.

d. Promote and distribute the carers' leaflet (FB31) more effectively.

e. Target and encourage ICA take-up amongst specific groups of carers, particularly those who are looking after children, elderly relatives or their spouses.

Chapter 5 Providing Information and Advice

In this chapter we consider the ways in which people obtain benefit information and their views about existing methods of dissemination. It is clear that some sectors of the disabled population remain poorly informed about the benefits to which they are entitled. In recognition of this alternative methods of providing benefit and related information are made.

5.1 Awareness and sources of information

Claimants obtain information about benefits from a wide variety of sources, although primarily in a very unsystematic way. Sources may include:

- the 'grapevine' – other people, including family, friends and acquaintances;
- general media sources, including newspapers, magazines, radio and TV programmes (such as 'The Money Programme', 'In Touch', and 'Does He Take Sugar?')
- specialist media sources including publications of disability groups (such as the Spastics Society's *Disability Now*);
- talking newspapers and books;
- voluntary organisations at both national and local levels;
- health and social services professionals;
- DSS/BA sources including leaflets and telephone helplines.

Despite the range of materials available and the considerable number of outlets through which benefit information is made available, a feeling of uncertainty about benefits and a sense of being ill-informed remains amongst disabled people and carers. In some instances people rely on informal sources for information (e.g. the grapevine) – they do not seek information, help or advice in an organised way. This occurs for a number of reasons:

- lack of awareness of available sources of benefit-related information. Although respondents may have been aware of local CAB services, for example, there was less certainty about their role in providing benefit information. Awareness of telephone advice lines (whether DSS or DIAL,[1] for example) was low; some people were not aware of specialist advice organisations, even those set up to provide wide ranging support, help and advice to people with specific disabilities;
- a feeling that DSS/BA staff, particularly front-line staff, are insufficiently expert in the range of disability benefits that are available;
- concern that staff (primarily DSS/BA) will not be experienced enough to cope with people with disabilities;
- not knowing whether there is anything to take advice about;
- lack of faith in the available sources of information, particularly DSS/BA;
- perceived problems in obtaining information from voluntary organisations. Because of growing workloads and squeezed funding there is a feeling that

1. DIAL – Disablement Information and Advice Line: a nationally based umbrella organisation with local services operating all over Great Britain.

voluntary agencies, such as CABx, are becoming more difficult to access. Some people talk of long waiting times; others of difficulties in getting through on the telephone;

- lack of confidence, or anxiety about approaching 'official strangers'; worries about displaying their ignorance;
- a vague assumption that they will automatically receive their full benefit entitlement – '... *the DHSS must know about me; I've sent in sick notes for long enough, so they must – well, I suppose they must – be giving me all I'm due.*'
- some people do not feel able to seek out the required information because of certain aspects of their disability. These may include problems of mobility, communication problems (hearing, sight or speech), anxiety and depression, and learning difficulties.

5.2 Methods of disseminating information – views and experiences

In this section we consider claimants' views and experiences of a number of existing materials that DSS/BA use to disseminate benefit information. These include leaflets, tapes (audio and video), telephone helplines and general publicity.[2]

Leaflets

Despite the length of time since the FB28 leaflet ('Sick or Disabled?') had been published (1988), awareness was low. This was also the case for leaflet FB31 ('Caring for Someone'), although this leaflet was published only a few weeks before the second stage of the study's fieldwork. Reasons for lack of awareness fell into four main categories. For some, there appeared to be problems of distribution – they had simply never seen the leaflets displayed, or the leaflets displayed were out of date. Others had low expectations of leaflets in general, and particularly those issued by government departments; as a result they had not looked for the information leaflets. A further problem seems to be salience; there are many leaflets displayed in public on a wide range of subjects resulting in difficulty in registering what there is and what might be relevant to the individual. FB28 also suffers from the problem that some people with disabilities do not identify with the label 'sick or disabled' – the title of the FB28 leaflet. This label tends to be less salient for people, as previously discussed (Section 3.1).

Reactions to both the FB28 and FB31 leaflets tended to be favourable, although rarely enthusiastic. In general, claimants felt that they would have liked to have had them; some thought that they might have avoided problems if they had had something of this nature at an earlier stage.

Large print leaflets can be very helpful to partially sighted people – indeed people with 'average' vision find larger type sizes easier to read. However, the size of type needed varies according to the type and severity of the visual impairment; there was a general feeling that the type size used in the new DLA claim packs was not nearly large enough for most people's needs. Some organisations for the visually impaired have CCTV which throws a very large image of a small section of printed material onto a screen. Although a rather slow method of reading leaflets, this can sometimes help people who otherwise could not read printed material.

Similarly, leaflets produced in Braille are useful to a minority of claimants, although it should be recognised that many visually impaired people – particularly those whose sight deteriorates late in life – are unable to use Braille.

With moves in recent years to empower people with learning difficulties, there is a continuing need for greater financial choice and independence. Existing materials

2. It should be noted that in some instances respondents were being exposed to some of these methods of disseminating information for the first time. In such cases we asked people how they felt about the 'concept' and whether they felt, after fairly brief exposure, it would meet their needs.

were felt to be too complex for this particular group of claimants; some carers and advisors felt that simpler materials would be of benefit to people with learning difficulties, as well as people who have difficulties with reading.

'It's the words they use. I can tell you why they are difficult for [son with learning difficulties] because they're not the words that come to normal conversation.' (Carer)

RECOMMENDATION 14

a. Check and improve distribution/display of literature.

b. Improve visibility and image of literature.

c. Raise expectations about the value of literature.

d. Consider providing leaflets in alternative formats, such as Braille.

e. Consider developing less complex materials for people who experience problems with reading.

***Audio and video tapes*[3]**

Awareness and experience of benefit information on audio and video tapes was low; some visually impaired respondents had received benefit information tapes through their talking newspapers. In some instances they were recognised as being similar, if not the same as, the DSS audio tapes; in others they were said to be completely different.

We were able to play extracts from these tapes to almost all of the Stage 2 respondents. Responses to the small extracts which were played to people tended to draw good, and sometimes enthusiastic, responses. This was so not merely among blind and partially sighted people, for whom sound tapes have an obvious relevance, but also amongst claimants with disabilities in general.

Positive features of the tape media included:

- tape, both audio and video, is almost like a personal explanation; people do not have to worry about reading or structuring the material themselves – they can let it 'unroll' in front of them;
- greater independence for people with visual impairments;

  'After listening to your tape I thought it was good, because with a tape you can always stop it and go back over it again. Besides if you have somebody come in, and they read you something, they might be in a hurry to go; you might not catch everything they read so you might have to wait a long time again for somebody to come in and read the same thing over to you again .... I think a tape would be marvellous actually, I really do, especially for people that are on their own.' (Claimant)

  'They're good guidelines, you can actually listen to it in total, and then go back over the relevant parts that you feel are suitable to you. And it gives confidence to people with visual handicap because you have the control. You are not feeling dependent on anyone having to go through it over and over again.' (Advisor)

- greater confidence that they would be able to understand audio- and videotape material compared to leaflets:[4] a view held by both the sighted as well as those who had visual impairments;

---

3. Audiotapes FB19 ('Social Security Benefits, a Guide for Blind and Partially Sighted People') and DS706 ('DLA guide'); and videotape 'DLA/DWA Explained'.
4. It should be noted that it was not the intention of the study to test the materials in detail, but rather to explore the 'concept'. Respondents' views that they would have less difficulty in absorbing and understanding information presented on tape may not necessarily hold true in practice.

- Videotaped material, in particular, is seen as potentially useful in helping people to realise that they might be eligible for benefits where their circumstances might make this less predictable. The DLA/DWA video, for example, shows people with a wide range of disabilities making a claim for benefit. The ability to give real examples of people with different types of disability on videotape, which people can identify with, was seen in a very positive light.

  'Some of the forms they send and the leaflets, I don't understand them, full stop. But now I thought that were brilliant [DLA videotape]. That were really good. Explains everything and you can understand it. You can follow it, and you knew what they were talking about, whereas in leaflets you're reading it and you're trying to fathom it out. I found it a lot better'. (Claimant)

While both the audiotape and videotape media were enthusiastically embraced, the appeal of videotape amongst sighted people was explained by its familiarity – there was a feeling that having pictures as well as words made it easier to absorb complex material.

There are, however, some disadvantages to 'taped' material:

- Not all claimants may have playback equipment, although *Social Trends* indicates that penetration of audio and video equipment into the home is reasonably high.[5]

- Tape is a serial medium which makes it harder to scan or skip irrelevant sections, or reprise what has already been heard. An information pack comprising a tape and a synopsis leaflet may help to overcome this.

  'You know the tape you're playing through, and when you miss bits you're winding back and you don't get back to where you want it to, whereas with a brochure if you get halfway down and you think, "I don't quite understand this bit," and you go back to the next paragraph, you know, the previous paragraph, and you pick it up again and you come through.' (Claimant)

- Both the audio and the video tapes were fairly long – the video tape was around 20 minutes in length, the audio tape (FB19) around an hour long. There is some concern that long, detailed presentations of complex benefits (particularly involving long lists) may be harder to assimilate than they sound. Better methods of presentation, it was felt, would overcome this. There may also be scope for presenting information in the form of a dialogue, or questions and answers, rather than simply reading long lists of information.

  'I think the problem with video is that it goes in and then goes straight out the other ear, but if you can get short messages across it will stick in people's minds, and then put the bulk of the information in leaflets. And, of course, so long as those leaflets are advertised in the video [it would] encourage people to go and get them. But if it just blurted out, "You can get this and this and this," all too fast, people just don't listen; it's almost like it just doesn't register.' (Claimant)

  'You will find that across the consensus of blind people, how it sounds is very important. It shouldn't be because you should accept that it's information, full stop. But if you're listening to some very complicated instructions or rules and regulations there's nothing worse than having the wrong voice. I mean they were speaking far too fast, far too fast. And the girl commented about the Freephone. She said, "You'll find it under ..." sounded like S not F. The intonation was very, very poor and that is quite critical; the tone of the voice is very important. Mustn't be

5. 53% of households have a video-player (*Social Trends*, 1991, HMSO).

a drony tone, and the high pitched one of the girl there would be very, very laborious. The gent would probably be OK if he spoke slower. The tone indexing was too loud.' (Claimant)

'I thought it started off nice, "If you're under 65;" that was fine – I was with them. Then it says, "But you can also claim if you're one day under 66 maybe." Then it goes on to say, "If you're over –," and I think with these various conditions the language gets very complicated.' (Advisor)

- The distribution of tapes was considered to require considerable thought. In general, respondents felt that they would like to be able to borrow tapes, preferably free, or at minimal cost. This would mean opening up new channels of distribution through libraries, advice agencies, disability support groups, DSS/BA, local authority offices, video hire shops, hospital and surgery waiting rooms, Post Offices, etc.

  'No-one minds paying a small charge, or even free, if you could borrow it; something similar to a lending library probably controlled by the DSS itself, say in one of the local offices.' (Claimant)

- The importance of updating benefit information applies equally to audio and video tapes, for which methods would need to be sought.
- There was some concern that the cost of producing materials in tape format may not be justifiable in terms of the amount of increased benefit take-up that they create. In order to be able to justify the cost, it was felt that considerable thought should be given to the methods and quality of presentation used, together with their subsequent distribution.

RECOMMENDATION 15

a. Develop audio and video tape materials for delivering benefit information to:

- visually impaired claimants;
- all disabled claimants;
- consider accompanying audio-tape materials with simplified leaflets.

b. Explore possible co-operation with other organisations such as RNIB and Talking Book/Newspaper schemes.

c. Experiment with better styles of presentation (e.g. problem-based dialogue), rather than just reading leaflets onto tape.

d. Consider methods of distribution to:

- individual claimants;
- advice agencies and other relevant groups.

e. Publicise and promote their existence.

Telephone helplines *(Freeline and BEL)*

Awareness of the DSS/BA telephone helplines was low, particularly the Benefit Enquiry Line (BEL). This was so for all the groups of people interviewed – claimants, carers and advisors (particularly small-scale local organisations). Where there was some awareness, confusion between Freeline and BEL also existed.

'It's the best kept secret from us.' (Claimant)

Response to the concept of a telephone helpline[6] was generally very positive amongst claimants and carers. In discussing the features of BEL, those most liked were:

- that it specialises in disability benefits, partly because they felt they would be talking to someone with 'technical expertise', but also because they felt that they would receive a more helpful and sympathetic service from a specialist facility;

- the availability of form-completion. This was felt to be very good news, partly because forms are a *bête noire* for most claimants, but also because some people with disabilities find it very difficult, or impossible, to fill out forms. While some get help from carers or friends, this is not always satisfactory as it can threaten their privacy and independence;

  'I would get them to fill me forms in, I can tell you straightaway. I never know what to put on forms because there's always two ways of saying something isn't there?' (Claimant)

  'I could see my son perhaps coping with that because he is good on the phone, but a form will baffle him.' (Carer – her son has learning difficulties)

  'They can actually send you information in Braille and large print so we certainly do support the Benefits Enquiry Line. It certainly is a big step forward in the information that was previously available to visually impaired people.' (Advisor)

- from the videotape that people saw, BEL was seen to be helpful and friendly. Some people who said they were nervous about phoning their local benefit office nevertheless felt that they could, and would like to, use the BEL service;

- that BEL is free and alleviates the cost of phone calls to local or national offices for information.

  'And the fact of Freephone, then you don't mind really telling somebody just what is wrong [with you], 'cos sometimes it can take a bit of time to go all through when they ask you what you're getting and that sort of thing. It does take time and when you've got to monitor your phone calls and do so many a month.' (Claimant)

Perhaps the main disadvantage of BEL (as with Freeline) is that it does not have access to case-papers and can, therefore, only give general advice. This prevents it from having a full 'trouble-shooting' role, the absence of which was met with considerable disappointment.

Some of the advice agencies who had made use of BEL were critical that the service appeared to be 'hopelessly overloaded'. A claimant also added, *'Judging on past experience it's always gonna be as unobtainable as the other one [Freeline].'* Some also said that the form-filling facility was not always 'on-line' and meant that this service was handled by getting another office to ring back some days later, a feature that was unpopular.

> *'Our experience of the Benefit Enquiry Line, apart from actually getting through to it – [they] absolutely promised that they would have an extra 400 staff on the telephone, which I don't think has occurred to be honest. The main problem with that is the forms-completion, because they won't phone you back there and then, they just take your name and number, then they'll get somebody in the regional office to phone you back, which could be several hours or even a day later – which seems to defeat the object somewhat.'* (Advisor)

---

6. We showed respondents either a copy of the BEL leaflet (BEL 1.2), and/or a brief description of the service that we had prepared in association with the DSS. Sometimes participants also saw part of the DLA/DWA video which shows BEL in operation.

Other advice workers were concerned as to whether the information and advice provided by BEL was entirely accurate. For example:

> *'I got at least one piece of wrong information from the Benefits Enquiry Line. I was querying about the lower rates of either components, which, you know, I thought would lead to a disability premium, but a client had been specifically told by a DSS officer that this was not the case. So I rang the Benefits Enquiry Line to check and they said it wouldn't lead to a premium. But I was fairly sure it was wrong so I pursued it further. But a lot of people are going to get put off just at that first stage because they'll assume that the Benefits Enquiry Line know what they're talking about.'* (Advisor)

> *'On the occasions when I've rung them up they haven't really known what they're talking about. That's the impression I've got. I haven't used it for a long time because of that. When it first set up I didn't find it very helpful, whereas the ordinary DSS Freeline I think they will try.'* (Advisor)

A further problem is that the 'Benefit Enquiry Line for people with disabilities' is known by the acronym BEL, or just as 'Benefit Enquiry Line' which gives the impression that the service is generic rather than specialised. 'Disability Benefit Helpline' was suggested as an alternative that would give the helpline an improved and targeted image; any change would need careful handling in order not to cause confusion.

Telephone helpline services are important, but have their limitations as some respondents pointed out. Some claimants do not have telephones and cannot easily get to one. Others are unable, or unwilling, to talk on the phone, either for physical or psychological reasons. Similarly, although people with hearing impairments can use telephone helplines with the aid of 'Minicom', ownership of Minicom is, we are informed, still very restricted. While telephone services should be developed, they should not be seen as sufficient to meet all the needs for help and advice.

RECOMMENDATION 16

a. Clarify and re-brand BEL and Freeline services as distinct entities.

b. Promote BEL more energetically as:

- a specialised service for people with disabilities;
- able to complete forms;
- friendly, helpful, approachable;
- technically expert;
- a service to claimants, carers and advisors.

c. Help promote other helplines (such as DIAL) as complementary services.

General publicity

There was some awareness of benefits advertising, usually on television, sometimes in newspapers. The recent DLA campaign and the adverts for Family Credit were those that were primarily recalled, although with little detail.

Media advertising met with a mixed reaction by claimants, carers and advisors. While some felt that TV advertising was a very powerful medium through which to promote awareness and understanding of benefits, others were less sure and felt that the perceived considerable cost in making and running TV adverts could be better spent on making strategic changes to the benefit system.

> *'I think more information on the media would be helpful. Say the television, for example. Most people – disabled, old, young, the sick – people always watch the*

television. And the television is the quickest way of getting information across – television and radio, and probably the national newspapers, probably local newspapers, as well.' (Claimant)

'There must be an awful, huge amount of money going into things like the DLA television campaign and things like that, but I'm sure it didn't produce the kind of response that was actually warranted there for the amount of money that was spent.' (Advisor)

Concerns about the messages provided by the TV adverts and the times of their transmission were also apparent.

'If I can vaguely remember it, there's a bloke and he held up this booklet on the telly and he said, "Apply for this now if you're disabled." And that was it .... Yes, I think it should have given you a bit more information about it, a bit more help, because they just said, "for disabled". It could mean anything.' (Claimant)

'The television programme was laughable, wasn't it? It was very good – [but] it was on at 2 o'clock in the morning. It was an excellent programme, and when I saw it was going to be on I thought, "Right, I'll just watch this." And I looked in the paper, and it was on at 2 o'clock in the morning. I thought it was a misprint but it wasn't; it was 2 o'clock in the morning.' (Claimant)

5.3 Providing information and advice – ways forward

There is a general feeling that people do not systematically seek out disability benefit advice. Indeed, much of the information people have about disability benefits comes from personal contacts – with friends, relations, employers, voluntary or professional workers, or simply casual contacts. As there is still considerable reluctance to use DSS/BA sources, and other organisations are often unable to meet people's benefit information needs (either through lack of awareness or difficulties with accessing the organisation), the 'grapevine' has become a central source of information and one which might be used to good effect.

However, the grapevine sometimes seems to deliver misleading or incorrect information, and sometimes discourages people from applying for benefits for which they might have been entitled. There is considerable 'folklore' about claiming benefits. It is, therefore, essential to 'feed the grapevine', to make sure that accurate and relevant information is disseminated. Clearly, the better informed the public is in general, the better the grapevine will work. However, it is doubtful whether any general campaign would convert 'folklorists' to 'experts', primarily because the system is so complex. A more appropriate method of informing the grapevine was felt to be through 'signposting' local, specialist organisations that can provide disability-related benefit information, as well as through professionals that disabled people, carers and advisors are likely to come into contact with.

Providing information through health and other professionals

Health professionals – doctors, nurses, health visitors, paramedics, surgery receptionists – are an important part of the grapevine. Some health professionals were said to be very helpful, providing claim forms and giving general help and support; there were cases where benefit claims appeared to be initiated on the basis of a suggestion from a health professional.

However, some health professionals do not appear to play this role at all; others are said to be poorly informed and can dissuade a potential claimant on the basis of inadequate or incorrect information.

The situation is tantalising. People with disabilities often have contact with health professionals; sometimes this is extensive, but at other times this may be at the onset of a disability or where deterioration starts to occur – often likely points when benefits should be considered. This makes them a vitally important channel for providing information and encouraging individuals to consider what they might be entitled to. Yet, health professionals are themselves under severe time pressures and may not see benefit advice as part of their role. Some may take the trouble to obtain information and pass it on, and this is to be encouraged and facilitated. Others, however, may be reluctant to become involved in an area about which they may know little, when they have so many pressures of their own. It is unlikely that this situation would change radically unless health professionals were given some positive incentive to become involved in giving benefit advice.

A more appropriate course may be to ensure that there is a well-publicised source of benefit advice in each area that health professionals can make a referral to. The provision of simple 'signpost' cards that health professionals could give out or display could capitalise on the links that people with disabilities may have with this professional group. By this means it would also be possible to help their patients approach the issue of benefits, without themselves having to take the time and accept the responsibility of learning to become benefits advisors.

Waiting rooms in surgeries, clinics and hospitals were also widely seen as good places to display literature, and possibly show videos. The information provided could be leaflets and/or 'signpost' materials. Larger waiting rooms might be visited from time to time by liaison officers with stands or exhibitions. There was also some suggestion that the existing problems with such outlets for benefit advice – out-of-date and out-of-stock leaflets – could be removed by using teams of merchandisers whose role it is to maintain the displays.

> *'... certainly for GPs to initiate. Even if they had a few leaflets on their desk and say, "Well look, take that and read it, you could be entitled to it." They don't even have to know much about it themselves really; so they don't have to spend too much time keeping up with all the relevant stuff.'* (Claimant)

> *'Usually at doctor's you see out-of-date leaflets. One reasonable project would be to fund an updating service for leaflet racks in GPs, dentists or public places that people might go to. You see, someone in the surgery has got to order it and got to wait for it to come through, and has got to remember to clear it away; and when a new one comes in you actually need to have it done for you.'* (Claimant)

Similar methods of providing access to disability benefit advice might also be made available through other relevant professionals including staff at establishments offering services for people with disabilities (such as day centres, training workshops, etc.), schools, social workers, etc.

Outreach workers

Because some people with disabilities find mobility and/or communication a problem, home visits in these cases would be welcome. Some advisors felt that the number of visiting officers (DSS/BA) is so limited that these have virtually disappeared, and few claimants or carers seemed to have much expectation of receiving one. Because of the perceived scarcity of visiting officers, respondents felt it would be hard to make a case for having one, even where their disability had severely restricted their abilities. Some advisors, in particular, argued that in such cases if the DSS/BA were not prepared to visit a person in their home, then they should be prepared to provide transport and help (in similarity with hospitals and day centres).

In some instances, advice agencies have been visited by DSS/BA staff. While this was welcomed in principle, for some, the perceived lack of expertise reduced the usefulness of the visit. Nevertheless, there seems to be considerable scope for extending the liaison officer function – going out to groups of elderly and disabled people attending day-time provisions, visiting advisors, offering training, seminars and courses to voluntary sector benefit advisors. This would both build up the voluntary sector's reputation and confidence as benefits advisors. However, there was some commentary about the way in which this should be managed; advisors wanted genuine benefits advice from experienced, expert, liaison officers – some advisors were worried that this could merely become a public relations activity rather than a serious aid to disseminating information.

'Since almost all disabled people have to see their doctor, their GP at some time or continually, would it be an idea if doctors surgeries were targeted with information and, possibly even on a rotation basis, to have somebody from the DSS, somebody who's roving who could go to different surgeries. In such and such a surgery there will be somebody from the DSS on Monday morning, so that people have one to one contact rather than trying to go and see or ring, which we have all agreed is a very difficult thing to do.' (Advisor)

'This idea of sending people out to do talks to local lunch clubs and things like that – that's really like a gloss on top. It's, "Aren't we doing a lot of stuff," good PR, which is next to useless. Changes have got to be integrated in the day-to-day running of each office. The training needs to be longer, more effective, of DSS staff – disability ones.' (Advisor)

RECOMMENDATION 17

a. Provide health professionals and other relevant workers with simple 'signposting' materials.

b. Exploit possibilities of waiting rooms and surgeries for information delivery via:

- literature displays;
- audio and video tapes;
- liaison officer visits and displays.

c. Promote, maintain and regularly update public leaflet displays.

d. Encourage, and resource, more liaison officer outreach through:

- home visits;
- visits to relevant disability-related groups;
- visits, seminars, and training for advisors.

Providing 'what-to-do' information

Current literature and tapes largely appear to concentrate on **providing information about the benefits themselves**, and the way they work. While such information is important, it is clear that, given the complexity of the benefits system in its present form, it is difficult for people to deal with information of this nature. Even where claimants can understand the principle of the benefit information they find it difficult to apply to themselves, because very detailed knowledge may be required. A person may understand a particular benefit in outline, therefore, but still be unable to make a decision as to whether they are likely to be eligible.

An alternative approach to the provision of detailed benefit information – as at present – would be to provide information that does not set out to be a tutorial on a complex system, but **which tells people what they should do** in a given situation, such as:

- what they might claim;
- where to get help and advice;
- how to proceed; and

- what to do if they experience problems, such as delays in the processing of the benefit, an unfavourable decision, a failed claim, etc.

This approach would simplify the range of benefit materials needed for the general public by providing 'signposts into the system', rather than a detailed exposition of the system itself.

RECOMMENDATION 18

Consider providing information and literature which:

- tells people what to do and where to go; rather than
- how each benefit works.

Chapter 6 Advice Agencies

6.1 The role of advice agencies

The term 'advice agencies' covers a wide spectrum of organisations with large variations along a number of dimensions. For example:

- **geographical coverage:**

  national v. local;

- **type and coverage of advice:**

  general advice on a wide range of topics v. specialist advice on a narrower range of topics;

- **client group:**

  - *other advice agencies v. general public;*
  - *disability-related v. general population;*

- **philosophy of organisation:**

  pressure group v. one-to-one advice and counselling;

- **nature of organisation:**

  sophisticated, technically expert information provider v. low key, ad hoc, information and advice;

- **funding:**

  grant-aided v. self-funded.

The role of advice agencies differs widely, according to the nature of the organisation, its philosophies, aims, client groups and levels of funding.

In terms of providing benefit information and advice, there are striking differences amongst the agencies in the types of advice they are able to provide (often due to their level of resources and facilities for training). At one end of the spectrum, nationally based agencies may have considerable insight into the way social security works, with some of the more specialist agencies having in-depth knowledge of the benefits system, including issues arising out of recent case law. At the other end of the extreme, many of the small local groups, particularly those that are non-specialist, and providing general advice and support, seem to know little more about the social security system than the people they are advising. In these latter instances, benefit advice may also be a peripheral interest to a group which is mainly set up to support people with a specific disability. Organisations such as these are often faced with a dilemma – they want to provide help, but feel (and often are) ill-equipped to do so. Funds are also under serious pressure (particularly at present), and will not stretch to training – or sometimes even to buying an up-to-date version of the *Disability Rights Handbook*.

Increasingly, advice agencies are seen as being overloaded with enquiries and not as responsive to a person's needs as they have been in the past. But there also continues to be some people who are either not aware of the role that local advice agencies can play in providing benefit information or advice, or choose not to seek advice in any systematic way (discussed fully in Chapter 4). The first objective must, therefore, be for the DSS/BA to decide whether the demand for disability benefit information and advice should be stimulated any further. Decisions about the ways in which this demand should be met can then be made; should the DSS/BA increase its role as information provider, or would greater funding of the voluntary sector be a more efficient use of resources?

In this respect, there seems to be considerable scope, and support, for partnership between DSS/BA and the voluntary sector. An initial task would be to identify and designate in each area a few key centres of disability benefit expertise (perhaps along the line of federations that currently exist in some areas); and a larger list of other possible sources of benefit information. Partnerships between DSS/BA and the voluntary sector were also felt to be worthwhile at both the national and local levels.

Advice agencies currently provide a wide range of services, from distributing benefit leaflets and forms, to being 'trouble-shooters' and 'problem-solvers'. This has a major impact on the way in which advice agencies are promoted (or 'signposted') in the community, the levels of technical expertise required by the advice agency workers, and the nature of their information requirements.

6.2 Providing 'signposts' to disability benefit advice

Considerable effort, it was felt, needed to be put into the promotion of local 'centres of disability benefit excellence' so that these key centres become known as the place to go for benefit and related information. This could be accomplished through the usual promotional channels – leaflets, local newspapers, local radio, etc., as well as simple 'signposting' methods. These should:

- encourage people to think about whether they might be entitled to benefits;
- publicise local sources of information and advice (DSS/BA and voluntary sector) and encourage their use;
- encourage and legitimise the idea of claiming;
- (perhaps) give broad indicators about likely entitlement.

RECOMMENDATION 19

a. Encourage co-operation and partnership between DSS/BA and the voluntary sector.

b. Identify key sources of advice about disability benefits (both DSS/BA and voluntary sector) at the local level.

c. Provide support for key voluntary sector advice agencies, at a local level, through publicity and resources (including benefit training).

6.3 Agencies' information needs

In this section we consider the type of information that agencies need, in terms of level of technical complexity and preferred formats and media. A number of issues also arose in this context concerning the dissemination of information from national organisations (including DSS/BA) to agencies operating at local level.

The technical complexity of materials

The information needs of agencies vary enormously. At one end of the spectrum, agencies who are providing simple, low level advice require benefit information and guides that give a broad indication of the benefits available, basic eligibility criteria and an indication of local organisations where advice of a more sophisticated nature could be found. The emphasis here is on simplicity of use. At the other end of the scale, both national organisations and some local agencies (particularly those with national links) require very high level and finely-tuned information (sometimes including fully detailed regulations as well as case law) in order that they can deal with cases which are often very complex or the subject of a dispute.

> *'If you want to contradict a decision appeal, you've got to get the law and you've got to get it right .... Not only do you need the regulations, you also ideally need to have the case law on those regulations, to have the commissioners' decisions available. And coming in some kind of accessible form. And not to have to pay vast amounts of money for it because you don't have enormous amounts of money.'* (Advisor)

During the course of the study, we presented advice workers (both formal and informal) with a wide range of existing materials for discussion. These included:

- basic leaflets, such as FB28 and FB31 (DSS/BA);
- technical guides in the HB and DS series (DSS/BA);
- Local Office Advice File (LOAF – DSS/BA);
- Benefit Advice Package (BAP – DSS/BA);
- materials produced by the Disability Alliance (*Disability Rights Handbook*) and Child Poverty Action Group (*National Welfare Benefits Handbook*).

Reactions to the various materials presented were varied, and dependent on the needs and the clientele of the advice agencies. The materials produced by voluntary organisations were well regarded, and met many of the information needs of all but the most sophisticated advisors. Smaller organisations that provided information on an informal and ad hoc basis sometimes felt that these publications were over-complicated for their use; the basic leaflets, such as FB28 and FB31, however, were felt to be too brief and simple.

Participants were interested to see copies of the LOAF and BAP files. Few were aware that these materials existed and could not see why they had not been made available to advisors. Views about these two sets of materials were varied. Some of the more sophisticated advisors saw them as being too general and brief to be of significant use to them; but others (particularly the less sophisticated local groups) felt they would be a useful source for quick reference by providing a guide to the range of benefits available.

Overall, the HB series of guides produced by DSS/BA found little favour with advice workers. They were felt to be insufficiently detailed for the majority of users, but too detailed and insufficiently concise for those advisors who required a quick and simple guide to the system of social security benefits. The technical accuracy of booklet HP5 was also questioned.

None of the materials met the needs of the most sophisticated advisors – their requirements included the detailed regulations as well as up-to-date case law.

DSS/BA information is found to be interesting mainly because it informs advisors what the system is actually working to. Advisors felt that DSS/BA information was sometimes suspect, in part, it was felt, due to inaccuracies, and in part because the available information did little to help claimants maximise their benefit entitlement – '*It's [the information] deliberately obtuse, so people don't find out what they're entitled to.*' Advisors also felt that it was useful to know what guidance is given to local office staff because this can then be quoted to officials in particular cases. If both sides have access to the official guidance then they start on a 'level playing field'.

Formats and media

The requirement for benefit information materials to the produced in a range of formats is dependent on the agencies use of the materials. Those advice workers who required information that could be given directly to the public felt that a variety of media were required including leaflets (in both standard and large-type formats), information produced in Braille and on audio cassettes.

Written materials

For use by the agencies themselves, a number of alternative formats were felt to be appropriate. *The Disability Rights Handbook* (Disability Alliance) was considered to be a useful format as it combined a depth of information with ease of use.

The formats of LOAF and BAP files created some interest amongst advisors; while there were mixed views about the amount of detail that was presented, the formats were favourably received. Some who were involved in home visits liked the portability of the LOAF format (Filofax-style), while others felt that the BAP cards (card index) would get lost or misfiled. On the other hand, the card index approach was felt to be very suitable for desk use.

> *'That [BAP] would be handy for the library, but then I get phone calls at home, and I can't carry everything at home.'* (Advisor)
>
> *'I think that's [BAP] pretty helpful; they could then update them.'* (Advisor)
>
> *'I don't think they have enough information in anyway. They're very, very vague as well .... They strike me as being very superficial .... I wouldn't expect somebody to be advised correctly if they were relying on this. There's no way somebody would get what's due to them .... There's one sentence on the Social Fund .... I've got Disability Working Allowance in front of me, and if this is advice supposedly being given dispassionately, it doesn't mention potential factors that need to be taken into account, in better-off calculations, such as going from maybe an incapacity benefit and Income Support, and losing mortgage interest as part of your applicable amount.'* (Advisor)

Regular updating was also a cause of some concern.

In the version of BAP that was initially used there was a topic index that was based on different 'groups' of claimants such as 'the elderly' and 'people with low incomes', etc., and suggested which benefit cards should be consulted. This seemed extremely useful, but was not available for the sets of BAP cards we were subsequently provided with by DSS/BA to show advisors.

Because the structure of disability benefits is complex we looked for a simple diagnostic system which could be used by advice workers (or conceivably by claimants themselves) to steer people in the right direction.

This might have been a simple device like a 'ready reckoner' or flow chart, or something more elaborate (like a computer routine or interactive video). DSS were not able to provide any new materials to work with, so we looked briefly at two existing examples, the BA/Royal College of Nursing 'Benefits wheel' and a pair of software-based benefit calculation routines.

Computer-based benefit calculation packages

Computer-based software packages are an alternative route to providing benefit information to advice agencies. We were loaned copies of two existing packages[1] which we were able to demonstrate briefly to advisor participants. Awareness of such programmes was limited, particularly amongst the smaller, less sophisticated advice organisations. Views were mixed about their potential usage.

1. Referred to as 'Ferret' and 'Jarman'. See Appendix B for details.

The perceived advantages[2] of using software-based systems were:

- they could be used by people without extensive knowledge of the benefit system;
- the ability to try 'what-if' scenarios;
- the ability to try 'better-off' calculations;
- results of the calculations could be printed out.

Perceived disadvantages included:

- lack of availability of suitable hardware;
- potential cost of providing hardware;
- cost of software, including updates;
- computer-phobia – some advisors felt reservations about using computers;
- fears that a computer would result in a 'de-skilling' of benefit advice workers to the detriment of the end user;
- the belief that 'a computer is always right'; a reluctance to challenge a computer's verdict;
- computers are perceived to be slow to use.

Despite these mixed feelings some felt that computer routines could become a valuable tool (rather than a replacement) for human advisors. Advisors argued, however, that there would be a need to be a 'corporate initiative' from the DSS/BA before increased use was likely to occur, primarily because of advice agencies' limited resources. It is hard to make a firm recommendation – the medium-to-long-term potential seems considerable through the computer's ability to handle complex systems, but so do the short-to-medium-term problems. No doubt these facilities will develop to some extent without DSS/BA intervention, but probably very slowly and in a piecemeal way. DSS/BA is the obvious player who could give this development a serious push.

> *'It's got a lot of potential providing it's a good package .... It's also important if they did develop it that the servicing of it is very good, because whenever a benefit changes, it's got to be instantly updated otherwise you'll be getting into a quagmire.'* (Advisor)

> *'No matter how good your computer package is, it's not going to replace someone who's had experience in advising on benefits. It could be a danger that if somebody goes through the package and the answer is no, then they'll assume that it's no because the computer package cost them a lot of money .... But some people just get a gut feeling that it's wrong and they actually try and ask some more questions, and try and go at it from a different angle.'* (Advisor)

> *'The idea that the DSS will fund a kind of library of computer terminals or whatever [is unlikely] at the same time as funding is being slashed for CAB, for Law Centres, for groups like DIAL all over the place.'* (Advisor)

2. It should be noted that reactions to the benefit calculation programmes were often based on limited experience or evaluation.

Benefits wheel

The 'benefits wheel' is a circular cardboard device (see Figure 1) which lists claimant groups around the circumference. The user lines up a slot in the wheel with the desired user group, and can then read off, for each of a list of benefits, which ones are 'Worth claiming', 'Unlikely', or for which the potential claimant should 'Seek Advice'.

In principle this was felt to provide just the kind of information many claimants needed but in practice seemed too vague to act as much more than a check list – the benefits wheel was felt to indicate 'Seek advice' ratings in too many instances.

Figure 1 Benefits wheel

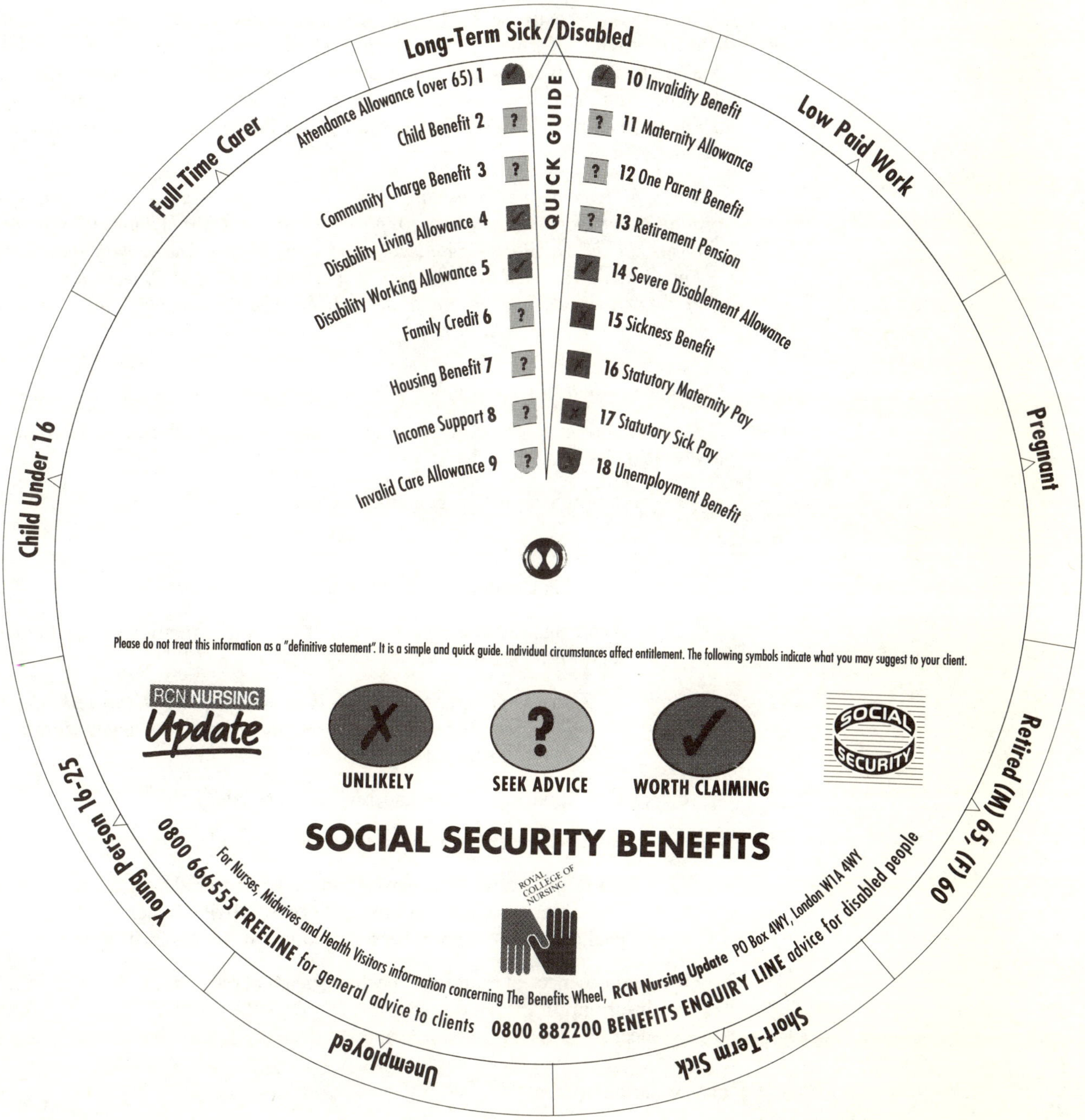

Although a useful and simply executed concept, the general feeling was that the Benefit wheel was too limited and general to be of any use to advisors, although some acknowledged that it might provide a useful 'signpost' for other professionals.

Telephone helplines

For some advice workers, telephone helplines (Freeline and BEL) had been a useful source of benefit advice and information, although primarily in 'cases of emergency or where clarification was sought. However, their comments about the usefulness of helplines as they currently exist were largely similar to those of claimants who had used them.

Views about the production of 'new' advice materials

There was a general concern, expressed amongst the advisors, that limited resources could easily be wasted on what some saw as 'window dressing' (in the form of issuing information in a variety of innovative media, free software, etc.) instead of either tackling the strategic issues – simplifying the system, improving efficiency and accuracy, providing better training, etc. – or funding advice agencies at a local level who felt that they could put the limited resources available to more productive use.

> *'I'm slightly concerned regarding these Filofaxes and things – if they [DSS/BA] all of a sudden decide after your report goes in that it's a brilliant idea, and they target all the voluntary organisations with these, you know, with these things. I'm slightly concerned over the cost of it all, which really will probably come out of the benefits that people would actually have to be receiving. And that sort of slightly worries me.'* (Advisor)

The dissemination of benefit information to advice workers

Three issues arise in the context of providing benefit and related information to advice agencies:

- obtaining supplies of benefit materials:
  - lengthy delays;
  - being sent materials that had not been ordered;
  - receiving insufficient supplies (this was mentioned particularly in relation to DLA/DWA)

    > *'They don't update it, and then when I sometimes ask them to update something, they send me something completely different to what I've asked for.' (Advisor)*

- regular updating of new and revised materials:
  - delays in receiving new and revised materials;
  - fears that any 'innovative' advisory materials that might be made available by DSS/BA (e.g. LOAF, BAP, benefit advice software packages) would soon become redundant unless swiftly updated.
- the absence of suitable mechanisms whereby both national and local information providers can inform DSS/BA of their benefit information needs.

RECOMMENDATION 20

a. Production of simple advisors guide:

- make LOAF and BAP available in short to medium term;
- consider longer term needs of advisors.

b. Consider future of technical leaflets (e.g. HB series) – discontinue or revise in consultation with advisors.

c. Consider publishing a 'high level' compendium of regulations and case law, regularly updated.

d. Consider the development of an 'advisors help-line'.

e. Improve distribution and updating of information and literature to advisors.

f. Develop mechanisms by which advisors, at both national and local level, can inform and discuss with DSS/BA their information needs.

g. Review the need to promote computer packages for advisors; consider:

- endorsing one or more software packages;
- funding hardware in whole or in part;
- funding software in whole or in part;
- provide and/or fund software package training;

h. Provide free/low cost benefits training.

Appendices

Appendix A Profile of Respondents

Claimants: a profile

Total claimants	68
Sex	
Female	40
Male	28
Age	
Under 20	5
20–29	12
30–39	11
40–49	17
50–59	13
60+	10
Marital status	
Single	23
Married/living as married	31
Divorced/separated	12
Widowed	2
Employment status	
Full-time work	3
Part-time work	–
Full-time education	4
Part-time education	2[1]
Day centre	1
Unemployed – looking for work	3
Unemployed – not looking for work	1
Permanently sick/disabled	53
Retired	1
Housing tenure	
Own	23
Rented – local authority	20
Rented – private	3
Housing association	3
Tied	1
Living with parents	16
Group home	2
Nature of disabilities	
Mobility	36
Sensory	23
Mental health	13
Learning difficulties[2]	2
Other (e.g. epilepsy)	19
Total	**93**[3]

1. One respondent attending a day centre for 2 days a week and part-time education for 3 days a week.
2. With the exception of two people with mild learning difficulties, the remainder were proxy interviews.
3. Number of disabilities is greater than number of claimants as some people reported more than one disability.

Age at onset of disability

Under 20	24[1]
20–29	9
30–39	14
40–49	13
50–59	7
60+	1

1. Eight people were born with their disability.

Help and support received

	In the home	Help with benefits
No help	28	27
Some help	28	18
A lot of help	8	9
Complete help	4	14
Total	**68**	**68**
Family	37	31
Friends	5	2
Voluntary body	–	4
Statutory body	4[1]	7[2]
Employer	–	2
Other	1[3]	1[3]
Total	**47[4]**	**47[4]**

1. Social worker, etc.
2. Occupational therapist, GP, Social worker.
3. Privately paid home help.
4. Some people had more than one source of help.

Receipt of benefits

	Receiving	Waiting	Failed	Discontinued	Total
Attendance Allowance	15	1	5	3	24
Mobility Allowance	23	1	5	–	29
Invalidity Benefit	26	–	1	1	28
Severe Disablement Allowance	26	–	1	–	27
Industrial Injuries Disablement Benefit	2	2	2	–	6
Income Support *with* special needs premium	10	–	2	–	12
Income Support *without* special needs premium[1]	6	–	2	4	12
Housing benefit[2]	16	1	–	1	18
Community Charge Benefit[2]	26	–	1	–	27
Total[3]	**150**	**5**	**19**	**9**	**183**

1. Some respondents not aware if they were receiving the special needs premium. Where they were receiving Income Support they are included here.
2. Some respondents were unsure whether they were receiving these benefits.
3. Some respondents in receipt of more than one benefit.

Carers: a profile

Total carers	43[1]
Sex	
Female	32
Male	11
Age	
20–29	4
30–39	5
40–49	8
50–59	14
60+	12
Nature of carers' disabilities	
None	29
Mobility	8
Sensory	2
Mental health	3
Other	4
Total	46[2]
Receipt of benefits	
Invalid Care Allowance	29
Mobility Allowance	1
Severe Disablement Allowance	4
Income Support	10
Housing Benefit	4
Community Charge Benefit	6
None	16[3]
Total	**55[4]**

1. Includes four professional carers.
2. Two respondents specified more than one disability.
3. Four professional carers.
4. Some respondents were in receipt of more than one benefit.

Who carers were caring for

Total carers	**44**[1]
Sex	
Female	21
Male	23
Age	
0 – 9	2
10 – 19	5
20 – 29	16
30 – 39	7
40 – 49	4
50 – 59	3
60+	7
Nature of disability[2]	
Mobility	15
Sensory	10
Mental health	9
Learning difficulties	20
Other	5
Help given in the home	
No help	5
Some help	19
A lot of help	9
Complete help	11
Help with benefits	
No help	5
Some help	3
A lot of help	3
Complete help	33

1. One person was caring for two people, the remainder were caring for one person.
2. Some people had more than one disability.

Appendix B Further Methodological Details

Sample selection

The sample of claimants and informal carers was selected from seven areas of England and Wales using records held by local benefits offices. Areas were selected to achieve variety in terms of local office practice, type of locality (urban, rural), and types of labour market. Quotas determining the sample were drawn up to achieve variety in terms of demography and claim history, and included:

- type of disability
  - mobility problems
  - mental health problems
  - blind/partially sighted
  - deaf/partial hearing
  - 'other' health problems
- type of benefit claimed[1]
  - Attendance Allowance
  - Mobility Allowance
  - Invalidity Benefit
  - Severe Disablement Allowance
  - Industrial Injuries Disablement Allowance
  - Income Support with special needs premium
  - Income Support without special needs premium
- benefit claim history
  - successful claim
  - failed claim
- age of claimant
- sex of claimant

In anticipation of a high 'drop-out' rate for reasons such as ineligibility on the basis of the quotas applied, inability to make contact, or refusal, five times the number of cases required for interview were selected from the local office records. The sampling of claimants was carried out by local offices and co-ordinated by the DSS on our behalf.

1. The study began before the introduction of Disability Living Allowance (DLA) and Disability Working Allowance (DWA).

Information providers were also included in the sample. These ranged from national and local organisations, and included agencies that provide both information and advice (such CAB, DIAL, etc.) as well as groups representing people with specific disabilities.

Contact and approach

After selection, respondents (current or failed claimants and informal carers) were initially contacted by a letter from the DSS. This explained the purpose of the study and asked that those who did not wish to be included should notify the DSS within a set time period. People who were unwilling to take part in the study were withdrawn from the sample lists. The remaining names were passed to SCPR for approach. An initial contact was then made, either in person, by telephone or letter, to explain further the purpose of the study and to make an appointment for a depth interview or attendance at a group discussion.

People with mental health problems or learning difficulties were not invited to group discussions and were always interviewed on a one-to-one basis; where people with mobility difficulties were asked to attend a group discussion, care was taken to ensure ease of access and, where necessary, appropriate travel arrangements were made and paid for.

The interviews and discussions

The depth interviews and group discussions took place, respectively, in respondents' own homes or in a hired room (e.g. in a community centre) in the locality. About six people attended each group discussion. Group discussions lasted around 1½ hours, depth interviews around 1–1¼ hours. These were tape recorded throughout and transcribed verbatim for subsequent analysis.

Fieldwork was carried out in two stages. The initial stage was primarily concerned with looking at the process of claiming benefit and the difficulties that people with disabilities experience. In the second stage interviews, the emphasis was primarily on a search for solutions to the problems identified earlier.

Interviews with claimants and carers were conducted in two parts. The initial part of the interviews, taking up to 15 minutes to complete, used a structured questionnaire to obtain background information such as household composition, a brief outline of the person's disability, their employment history and the receipt of benefits. The major part of the interview used a topic guide and depth interview techniques to explore a range of issues surrounding the issue of making a claim of benefit. Subjects to be covered in the interviews were drawn up in consultation with the DSS/BA. Interviews were conducted around the topic guides which outlined the core issues to be explored with all respondents, but with flexible questioning to allow differences of experience and emphasis. Separate topic guides were designed and used with claimants, carers and representatives of disability-related organisations and agencies.

For the second stage interviews, a revised topic guide was designed, reflecting a 'solutions' emphasis, and used in conjunction with a wide range of stimulus materials. These included a number of purpose-designed show cards – shown later in Appendix C (page 81) – and a selection of materials drawn from those produced by the Benefits Agency and other organisations. They included:

- *Disability Rights Handbook* (Disability Alliance);
- *National Welfare Benefits Handbook* (Child Poverty Action Group);
- a range of Benefits Agency leaflets, including 'Sick or Disabled?' (FB28), 'Caring for Someone?' (FB31) and 'Benefit Enquiry Line' (BEL 1.2);
- a range of Benefits Agency guides, including 'A Guide to Non-contributory Benefits for Disabled People' (HB5), 'Disability Working Allowance –

Information for Advisers' (DS709) and 'An Introduction to Disability Living Allowance';

- 'Benefit Wheel' (Benefits Agency/Royal College of Nursing);
- 'Benefit Advice Package' (BAP) (Benefits Agency);
- Local Office Advice File (LOAF) (Benefits Agency);
- Videotape – 'For Your Benefit ... DLA/DWA Explained' (Benefits Agency);
- Audiotapes – 'Social Security Benefits ... A Guide for Blind and Partially-sighted People' (FB19 Cass), 'Guide to New Benefits for Disabled People' (DS706 Audio) and 'The Patient's Charter';
- Benefit calculation software – The Lisson Grove Welfare Benefits Program (Billen/Blackwell/Bruster/Jarman) and Maximiser Plus by Ferret Information Systems Ltd.[2]

Analysis

Based on both the tape recordings and the verbatim transcripts, a detailed content analysis of the qualitative data was carried out. Analytical charts were constructed, synthesising the attitudes and experiences of respondents in relation to each of the issues, identifying recurrent themes or patterns of association within the data. These charts, together with illustrative material taken verbatim from the interviews, forms the basis of this report.

2. Known as 'Jarman' and 'Ferret', respectively.

Appendix C
Fieldwork Documents

SOCIAL & COMMUNITY
SCPR
PLANNING RESEARCH

35 NORTHAMPTON SQUARE
LONDON EC1V 0AX
TELEPHONE 071-250 1866
FAX 071-250 1524
E-mail (Janet) : scpr @ uk.ac.city

Dear

Benefits Research

Thank you for agreeing to take part in this research study which is being carried out by Social and Community Planning Research (SCPR), an independent research institute, for the Department of Social Security (DSS).

The research is looking at the experiences of people who claim, or have tried to claim disability or illness-related benefits, either for themselves or on someone else's behalf. The purpose of the study is to help us better understand whether the information the DSS provides about benefits is the information you need in a way that you can use it. Having your views should help the DSS to provide you with a good quality service.

The interview will take the form of an informal discussion, with an SCPR interviewer, and should last for approximately 1¼ hours. Anything you say will be treated in the strictest confidence and used only for the purposes of the research. £10.00 will be paid to everyone who takes part to cover any inconvenience or expense.

We look forward to seeing you at .... am/pm on .... 1991 when an SCPR interviewer will come to talk to you.

Yours sincerely

Jill Keegan
Andrew Thomas
Researchers

SOCIAL & COMMUNITY
SCPR
PLANNING RESEARCH

35 NORTHAMPTON SQUARE
LONDON EC1V 0AX
TELEPHONE 071-250 1866
FAX 071-250 1524
E-mail (Janet) : scpr @ uk.ac.city

Dear

Benefits Research

Thank you for agreeing to take part in this research study which is being carried out by Social and Community Planning Research (SCPR), an independent research institute, for the Department of Social Security (DSS).

The research is looking at the experiences of people who claim, or have tried to claim disability or illness-related benefits, either for themselves or on someone else's behalf. The purpose of the study is to help us better understand whether the information the DSS provides about benefits is the information you need in a way that you can use it. Having your views should help the DSS to provide you with a good quality service.

The interview will take the form of an informal discussion, with a small number of people like yourself and an SCPR interviewer, and should last for approximately 1¼ hours. Anything you say will be treated in the strictest confidence and used only for the purposes of the research. £10.00 will be paid to everyone who takes part to cover any inconvenience or expense.

We look forward to seeing you at:

Venue: ....
Time: ....
Date: ....

Yours sincerely

Jill Keegan
Andrew Thomas
Researchers

P5173 TG1/1 **Stage 1**

Benefit information needs of people with long term sickness or disability

PRELIMINARY INTERVIEWS WITH NATIONAL AGENCIES

Background

- Role in organisation
- Responsibility for sick/'disabled' issues

Client Groups

- Who does the organisation deal with
  - are long term sick/disabled catered for specifically
- Contact with long term sick/disabled
  - methods of contact; difficulties with making contact
  - range of people making contact; eg physical disability, mental health, learning difficulties
  - any client groups not (adequately) covered

Services provided

- In general
- For long term sick/disabled

Disseminating benefit/service information

- Views about the ways in which benefit/service information is disseminated

- Problems arising; what are they
  - same/different for ALL benefits
  - same/different for ALL types of sickness/disability

- Why do such problems arise
  eg
  - nature of information available
  - complexity of information available
  - physical access to buildings
  - helpfulness of benefit office staff
  - complexity of benefit regulations
  - poor/inadequate targeting of information
  - availability of information on different media

The way forward

- What should be done to make benefit/service information more accessible

  - at a National level
  - at a local level
  - for different types of clients (eg disability)
  - for different types of benefits
  - using different types of media

- Views about recent initiatives (eg tapes, telephone help-line)
  PROBE familiarity
  perceived/known usefulness

P5173 Q1/2 Stage 1

Access to service and benefit information needs of sick and disabled people

Background questionnaire and checklist

Complete for every claimant and carer (not agencies)

ID ____________

CLAIMANT DETAILS

1. Sex
   - Female ☐
   - Male ☐

2. Age ____________

3. Marital status:
   - Single ☐
   - Married ☐
   - Living as married ☐
   - Separated ☐
   - Divorced ☐
   - Widowed ☐

4a. Number of people living in household: ________

4b. Who are they? How many?

	No.
Partner	____
Parents	____
Dependent children	____
Non-dependent children	____
Other relatives	____

5. Housing tenure
   - Own ☐
   - Rent - Local authority ☐
   - Rent - Housing association ☐
   - Rent - Private landlord ☐
   - Live with parents ☐
   - Other ____________

6. Ethnic origin
   - White ☐
   - West Indian ☐
   - Indian ☐
   - Pakistani ☐
   - Bangladeshi ☐
   - Chinese ☐
   - African ☐
   - Arab ☐
   - Mixed origin ☐
   - Other ____________

7a. Name of sickness/disability: ____________________

7b. Type of sickness/disability:

- Ambulatory/Mobility ☐
- Sensory ☐
- Learning difficulty ☐
- Mental health ☐
- Other ____________ ☐

7c. Subjective measure of extent of disability

- Mild ☐
- Moderate ☐
- Severe ☐

7d. Age at onset of sickness/disability ____________

8a. Employment status

- Full time work ☐
- Part time work ☐
- Government scheme ☐
- Full time education ☐
- Part time education ☐
- Unemployed - looking for work ☐
- Unemployed - not looking for work ☐
- Permanently sick/disabled ☐
- Looking after family/home ☐
- Retired ☐

8b. IF WORKING Type of work ____________

8c. IF PART TIME Number of hours ____________

9. Benefits. Ask about benefits
RECEIVED/APPLIED FOR AND AWAITING DECISION/FAILED APPLICATIONS/NOT APPLIED FOR BUT MIGHT BE ELIGIBLE/DISCONTINUED CLAIM

	Received	Waiting	Failed	Poss.	Discontinued
Attendance allowance					
Mobility allowance					
Severe Disablement allowance					
Invalidity Benefit					
Industrial Injuries Disablement Benefit					
Income Support with Special Needs Premium					
Income Support without Special Needs Premium					
Invalid Care Allowance					
Unemployment Benefit					
Housing Benefit					
Community charge benefit					

10. **Practical help**

a) Help received with daily household tasks, such as washing, dressing, cooking, housework, shopping, etc.

No help ☐
Some help ☐
A lot of help ☐
Complete help ☐

b) Who generally provides this help?

Family ☐
Friends ☐
Voluntary agency ☐
Statutory agency ☐

c) Help received with making benefit claims/dealing with DSS

No help ☐
Some help ☐
A lot of help ☐
Complete help ☐

d) Who generally provides this help?

Family ☐
Friends ☐
Voluntary agency ☐
Statutory agency ☐

****

CARER DETAILS (Complete only if a carer/claimant or Carer only interview)

1. Sex

   Female ☐
   Male ☐

2. Age ____________

3a. Name of sickness/disability: ____
    WRITE 'NONE' IF NO SICKNESS/DISABILITY

3b. Type of sickness/disability:

   Ambulatory/Mobility ☐
   Sensory ☐
   Learning difficulty ☐
   Mental health ☐
   Other ____________________ ☐

3c. Subjective measure of extent of disability

   Mild ☐
   Moderate ☐
   Severe ☐

3d. Age at onset of sickness/disability ____________________

4a. Employment status <u>OF CARER</u>

   Full time work ☐
   Part time work ☐
   Government scheme ☐
   Full time education ☐
   Part time education ☐
   Unemployed - looking for work ☐
   Unemployed - not looking for work ☐
   Permanently sick/disabled ☐
   Looking after family/home ☐
   Retired ☐

4b. IF WORKING — Type of work ____________________

4c. IF PART TIME — Number of hours ____________________

5. Benefits RECEIVED BY CARER. Ask about benefits
RECEIVED/APPLIED FOR AND AWAITING DECISION/FAILED APPLICATIONS/NOT APPLIED FOR BUT MIGHT BE ELIGIBLE/DISCONTINUED CLAIM

	Received	Waiting	Failed	Poss.	Discontinued
Attendance allowance					
Mobility allowance					
Severe Disablement allowance					
Invalidity Benefit					
Industrial Injuries Disablement Benefit					
Income Support with Special Needs Premium					
Income Support without Special Needs Premium					
Invalid Care Allowance					
Unemployment Benefit					
Housing Benefit					
Community charge benefit					

6. Relationship to claimant ____________________________

Benefit information needs of people
with long term sickness or disability

TOPIC GUIDE FOR CLAIMANTS & FAILED CLAIMANTS

Throughout the interview emphases should be placed on:

a) the effect of the respondents' specific difficulties in gaining access to the benefit system and their experiences of making a claim;

b) the effect of past experiences (of claiming) on subsequent/future claims;

c) potential solutions that will empower people with disabilities to make their own claims.

1. <u>Personal background</u>

From recruitment questionnaire
Check: Benefits received; inc. housing benefit, community charge benefit and other 'general benefits'
Employment status

2. <u>Nature of Sickness and Disability (inc. perceptions of disability)</u>

- Nature of Sickness/Disability (briefly)
  - nature of sickness/disability
  - how long have they had it/age of onset/when did it start to affect them
  - has it changed over time (how)

- Effects of Sickness/Disability
  PROBE: mobility; reading; communication; handling money; ability to work

- Personal support - provided
  i) generally (briefly)
  ii) with benefit claims
  Distinguish statutory and voluntary support
  PROBE: with mobility; communicating; reading forms; handling money

  - who helps them (relationship)
  - how long have they helped
  - feelings about help (especially with claims); eg control over money; trust; privacy; independence

- Personal support - needed
  i) generally (briefly)
  ii) with benefit claims

  - what sort

- Perceptions of sickness/disability
  - how do they see themselves; sick?; disabled; etc
  - would they read a leaflet that was marked for people who were 'sick' or 'disabled'

3. <u>Financial/Benefits Situation</u>
USE PROMPT CARDS

i) Recap benefits currently received

ii) Any benefits received in the past but now discontinued

iii) Any changes in levels of benefits, eg. change from higher to lower rate attendance allowance

iv) Any 'failed' claims

v) Considering making a claim

4. <u>Making a benefit claim</u>
NOTE: Take respondent through each benefit in turn, including CURRENT, DISCONTINUED, CHANGED, FAILED and CONSIDERED claims.

- Views about receiving benefits (eg. charity/entitlement); how can this change
  - effect of views on what they claim/when they claim

- Sources of information about benefits
  - how did they find out; had they heard about it before
  - why did they think they were eligible; any hesitations over eligibility eg. AA/MobA - don't need to be receiving help, just that they require help
  - any delays hearing about benefit and making a claim; reasons; solutions
  - any difficulties in obtaining documents to make a claim
  - does the name of a benefit:
    - i) affect whether they make a claim
    - ii) affect views about eligibility

- Seeking advice (formal/informal)
  - did they seek any (further) advice; why/why not
  - from whom did they seek advice
  - problems/advantages with obtaining advice from these sources
  - satisfaction with i) method of obtaining information
    ii) advice given
  - would they use source again
  - knowledge of other sources NOT USED; reasons for non use

- Making a benefit claim (recent claims - past 2 years - only)
  - did they know how to make the claim
  - expectations about what would happen; ie time taken to sanction claim; need for medical evidence; assessment; etc
  - who is involved in making a benefit claim
  - any help with making a claim

  IF HELP PROVIDED
  - does claimant feel in need of help, why/why not
  - degree of satisfaction with help being received; preferences about type of help needed (eg telephone call, visit to office, visit by DSS officer)
  - feelings about having help with claims
  - is this the person who should be helping; why/why not; who should help

  IF HELP NOT PROVIDED
  - does claimant feel in need of help; why/why not
  - is claimant satisfied with not receiving help; why/why not
  - knowledge of any help available; if so, feelings about help available
  - should there be help available; if so, what preferences about type of help needed (eg telephone call, visit to office, visit by DSS officer)

- The forms (relate to respondent's specific disabilities)

  Distinguish between the claim form and supporting information

  i) accessibility
  ii) presentation; formality; user friendly; typeface (size and style)
  iii) complexity of language; clarity of instructions; problems for non-English speakers or English as a second language
  iv) different formats; experience; preferences;
  v) presentation of supporting evidence required; clear; detailed
  vi) determining eligibility
  vii) problems for particular groups
  viii) other problems

- Experience of interviews/medical assessments
  - did they know what to expect; why/why not; how should they be informed
  - views about interviews/assessments
    i) treatment by staff
    ii) any difficulties with travel to/access to assessment/interview office
    iii) overall views about need for assessment; what would be fair; what alternatives would be preferable
    iv) overall views about how assessment/interview was handled
    v) offer of home visits?
    vi) effect of experience on subsequent/future claims

- Awaiting a response
  - time taken for claim to be approved; time taken to be paid
  - was payment backdated to date of claim
  - views about backdating
    - to date of claim
    - prior to claim

- Overview of claims process
  (briefly if already covered)
  - sources of information
  - the forms
  - the names of the benefits (ie affect views about whether eligible)
  - health checks
  - interviews
  - time taken to make claim
  - time taken to sanction claim

  ASK ALL
  - do they feel in control of the situation; why/why not
  - do they understand the claims process; why/why not
  - would they go through it again; why/why not

- Methods of payment; experience; preferred method; problems

- If things go wrong, why

5. <u>DISCONTINUED CLAIMS (if appropriate)</u>

- Details of discontinued claim(s)
  - why no longer receiving benefit
  - whose decision was it to discontinue claim
  - feelings about discontinued claim

6. <u>CHANGED CLAIMS (if appropriate)</u>

- Details of changed claim(s)
  - which benefit(s)
  - reasons for change; whose decision
  - knowledge of appeal process
  - did they take any action

i) what action taken (eg appeal)
ii) any help sought; what; who from; satisfaction
iii) outcome of action

- perceptions of appeal process
- feelings about changed claim

7. FAILED CLAIMS (if appropriate)

- Details of failed claim(s)
  - which benefit(s)
  - understanding of why claim failed

  PROBE: i) raised expectations (eg by doctors, friends, the way leaflets are written)
  ii) understanding of reasons given by DSS

  - did they take any action
    i) what action taken (eg appeal)
    ii) any help sought; what; who from; satisfaction
    iii) outcome of action

  - perception of appeals process
  - fairness of decision to turn down claim
  - would they i) make another claim in the future
    ii) appeal again in the future

8. Awareness of (other) Benefits (especially for eligible non-claimants)

- Awareness
  - are benefits they receive the only ones entitled to
  - perceptions of entitlement to other benefits (which)
  - where did they hear about them
  - how long have they known about them
  - reasons for any delay in applying
  - have they applied for them yet (why/why not)

  IF MADE A CLAIM
  - which have they applied for
  - when did they apply
  - what is the status of the claim
  - any problems with the claim (describe)

  IF NOT MADE A CLAIM
  - why haven't they applied (details)
  - do they expect to apply in future
  - what would it take to get them to apply

- Changes in health status
  - if health status changed
    i) would they know entitlement
    ii) how would they find out

9. The DSS

- Understanding of centrally/locally administered benefits
  - knowledge of how to find out about progress of claim

- Contact with the DSS (relate any difficulties to person's disabilities)
  - by what means; when would they use different methods
  - adequacy of contact; what are the problems; time taken to answer phone; no. of staff talked to; satisfactory resolution of problem
    time (and frequency)

quality of information
quantity of information; does DSS look at needs of <u>whole person</u>

- do they have a contact name in case of problems/queries; usefulness

- do they know who they are talking to; is it important to know; do they understand their role

- preferred type of contact with DSS - if DSS need to contact them how should they do t (phone/letter, etc)

- preferences for detailed notifications about decisions versus brief/letters with offers of more information

- Feelings about contacting the DSS
    - satisfaction with treatment received (describe)
    - degree of trust in dealing with DSS; do they <u>trust</u> the information provided
    - satisfaction with updating of information

- Image of DSS
    - attitudes towards the organisation
    - attitudes towards people there
    - perceived attitudes of DSS to claimants

- Feelings about Sick/Disabled Label
    - does it affect treatment received at DSS (how)
    - feelings about this
    - feelings about the label itself

10. <u>Awareness of Change - DSS/Benefits Agency (briefly)</u>

- Knowledge of changes in the DSS
    - the Benefits Agency
    - feelings about changes
    - satisfaction with communication about changes

- Knowledge of new benefits; DWA/DLA (briefly)

- Suggestions
    - how should changes be communicated

11. <u>Improvements Needed</u>

- How can DSS help:
    - them as individuals (describe)
    - people with disabilities similar to theirs
    - any people applying for these same kind of benefits

- Information about benefits; including using different media
    - complexity of benefits

- If improvements were made:
    - how should they be communicated (eg target versus general broadcast)

12. Awareness/Experience of Special Facilities for Sick/People with disabilities

- Have they heard of any special facilities for people with disabilities; eg wider doors, ramps; staff who can sign, staff visits to groups, tapes, etc. (what)
  - experience of using them
  - views about use

- Experience of using special facilities; satisfaction

- What special facilities would they like to use

- What would empower them to be more independent (in accessing and claiming benefits)?

P5173 TG3/4 Stage 1

Benefit information needs of people
with long term sickness or disability

TOPIC GUIDE FOR CARERS WHO ARE INVOLVED IN MAKING CLAIMS

Throughout the interview emphases should be placed on:

a) the effect of the respondent's specific difficulties in gaining access to the benefit system and their experiences of making a claim;

b) the effect of past experiences of claiming on subsequent/future claims;

c) potential solutions that will empower people with disabilities to make their own claims.

1. <u>Personal background of carer</u>

- Age
- Employment status; type of work; hours
- Relationship to sick/disabled person
- Do they think of themselves as a carer?
- Length of time in caring role
- Does anyone else help with caring?
- Are they the person who gives most support with benefit claims

2. <u>Background of person for whom care is provided</u>
Ask if not already collected in recruitment questionnaire
- Age
- Family composition
- Financial status; benefits received
- Employment status; type of work; hours
- Nature of Sickness/Disability (briefly)
    - nature of sickness/disability
    - how long have they had it/age of onset/when did it start to affect them
    - has it changed over time (how)

- Effect of sickness/disability; mobility; reading; communication; handling money; ability to work

3. <u>Role as Carer</u>

- Personal support - provided
  i) generally (briefly)
  ii) with benefit claims
  Distinguish statutory and voluntary support
  PROBE: with mobility; communicating; reading forms; handling money

  - who helps them (relationship)
  - how long have they helped
  - feelings about help (especially with claims); eg control over money; trust; privacy; independence

- Personal support - needed
  i) generally (briefly)
  ii) with benefit claims

- Perceptions of sickness/disability
  - how does carer see the person they care for; sick; disabled; etc
  - would carer read a leaflet that was marked for people who were 'sick' or 'disabled'

3. <u>Financial/Benefits Situation</u>
USE PROMPT CARDS

i) Recap benefits <u>currently</u> received

ii) Any benefits received in the past but now <u>discontinued</u>

iii) Any <u>changes</u> in levels of benefits, eg. change from higher to lower rate attendance allowance

iv) Any <u>'failed'</u> claims

v) <u>Considering</u> making a claim

4. <u>Making a benefit claim</u>
NOTE: Take respondent through each benefit in turn, including CURRENT, DISCONTINUED, CHANGED, FAILED and CONSIDERED claims.

- Views about receiving benefits (eg. charity/entitlement); how can this change
  - effect of views on what they claim/when they claim

- Sources of information about benefits
  - how did they find out; had they heard about it before
  - why did they think they were eligible; any hesitations over eligibility; eg AA/MobA - don't need to be <u>receiving</u> help, just that they <u>require</u> it
  - any delays hearing about benefit and making a claim; reasons; solutions
  - any difficulties in obtaining documents to make a claim
  - does the name of a benefit:
    - i) affect whether they make a claim
    - ii) affect views about eligibility

- Seeking advice (formal/informal)
  - did they seek any (further) advice; <u>why/why not</u>
  - from whom did they seek advice
  - problems/advantages with obtaining advice from these sources
  - satisfaction with
    - i) method of obtaining information
    - ii) advice given
  - would they use source again
  - knowledge of other sources NOT USED; reasons for non use

- Making a benefit claim
  - did they know how to make the claim
  - expectations about what would happen; ie time taken to sanction claim; need for medical evidence; assessment; etc
  - who is involved in making a benefit claim
  - any help with making a claim

  IF HELP PROVIDED
  - does carer feel in need of help, why/why not
  - degree of satisfaction with help being received; preferences about type of help needed (eg telephone call, visit to office, visit by DSS officer)
  - feelings about having help with claims
  - is this the person who should be helping; why/why not; who should help

  IF HELP NOT PROVIDED
  - does carer feel in need of help; why/why not
  - is carer satisfied with not receiving help; why/why not
  - knowledge of any help available; if so, feelings about help available
  - should there be help available; if so, what preferences about type of help needed (eg telephone call, visit to office, visit by DSS officer)
  - does carer feel they are the person who should be helping; who should help

- The forms (relate to respondent's specific disabilities)
  Distinguish between the claim form and supporting information
  - i) accessibility
  - ii) presentation; formality; user friendly; typeface (size and style)
  - iii) complexity of language; clarity of instructions; problems for non-English speakers or English as a second language
  - iv) presentation of supporting evidence required; clear; detailed
  - v) determining eligibility
  - vi) problems for particular groups
  - vii) other problems

- Experience of interviews/medical assessments
  - did they know what to expect; why/why not; how should they be informed
  - views about interviews/assessments
    - i) treatment by staff
    - ii) any difficulties with travel to/access to assessment/interview office
    - iii) overall views about need for assessment
    - iv) overall views about how assessment/interview was handled
    - v) offer of home visits
    - vi) effect of experience on subsequent/future claims

- Awaiting a response
  - time taken for claim to be approved; time taken to be paid
  - was payment backdated to date of claim
  - views about backdating - to date of claim
    - prior to claim

- Overview of claims process
  (briefly if already covered)
  - sources of information
  - the forms
  - the names of the benefits (ie affect views about whether eligible)
  - health checks
  - interviews
  - time taken to make claim
  - time taken to sanction claim

  ASK ALL
  - do they feel in control of the situation; why/why not
  - do they understand the claims process; why/why not
  - would they go through it again; why/why not

- Methods of payment; experience; preferred method; problems

- If things go wrong, why

5. <u>DISCONTINUED CLAIMS (if appropriate)</u>

- Details of discontinued claim(s)
  - why no longer receiving benefit
  - whose decision was it to discontinue claim
  - feelings about discontinued claim

6. <u>CHANGED CLAIMS (if appropriate)</u>

- Details of changed claim(s)
  - which benefit(s)
  - reasons for change; whose decision
  - knowledge of appeal process
  - did they take any action
    - i) what action taken (eg appeal)

ii) any help sought; what; who from; satisfaction
iii) outcome of action
- perceptions of appeal process
- feelings about changed claim

7. FAILED CLAIMS (if appropriate)

- Details of failed claim(s)
  - which benefit(s)
  - understanding of why claim failed
    PROBE: i) raised expectations (eg by doctors, friends, the way leaflets are written)
    ii) understanding of reasons given by DSS
    - did they take any action
      i) what action taken (eg appeal)
      ii) any help sought; what; who from; satisfaction
      iii) outcome of action

  - perception of appeals process
  - fairness of decision to turn down claim
  - would they i) make another claim in the future
    ii) appeal again in the future

8. Awareness of (other) Benefits (especially for eligible non-claimants)

- Awareness
  - are benefits they receive the only ones the person they care for is entitled to
  - perceptions of entitlement to other benefits (which)
  - where did they hear about them
  - how long have they known about them
  - reasons for any delay in applying
  - have they applied for them yet (why/why not)

  IF MADE A CLAIM
  - which have they applied for
  - when did they apply
  - what is the status of the claim
  - any problems with the claim (describe)

  IF NOT MADE A CLAIM
  - why haven't they applied (details)
  - do they expect to apply in future
  - what would it take to get them to apply

- Changes in health status
  - if health status changed
    i) would they know entitlement
    ii) how would they find out

9. The DSS/BA

- Understanding of centrally/locally administered benefits
  - knowledge of how to find out about progress of claim

- Contact with the DSS/BA (relate any difficulties to person's disabilities)
  - by what means; when would they use different methods
  - adequacy of contact; what are the problems; time taken to answer phone; no. of staff talked to; satisfactory resolution of problem

i) time (and frequency)
ii) quality of information
III) quantity of information; does DSS/BA look at needs of <u>whole person</u>

- do they have a contact name in case of problems/queries; usefulness
- do they know who they are talking to; is it important to know who they are talking to, do they understand their role
- preferred type of contact with DSS/BA - if DSS/BA need to contact them how should they do it (phone/letter, etc)
- preferences for detailed notifications about decisions versus brief letters with offers of more information

- Feelings about contacting the DSS/BA
  - satisfaction with treatment received (describe)
  - degree of trust in dealing with DSS/BA; do they <u>trust</u> the information provided
  - satisfaction with updating of information

- Image of DSS/BA
  - attitudes towards the organisation
  - attitudes towards people there
  - perceived attitudes of DSS/BA to claimants

- Feelings about Sick/Disabled Label
  - does it affect treatment received at DSS/BA (how)
  - feelings about this
  - feelings about the label itself

10. <u>Awareness of Change - DSS/Benefits Agency (briefly)</u>

- Knowledge of changes in the DSS/BA
  - the Benefits Agency
  - feelings about changes
  - satisfaction with communication about changes

- Knowledge of new benefits; DWA/DLA (briefly)

- Suggestions
  - how should changes be communicated

11. <u>Improvements Needed</u>

- How can DSS help:
  - them as individuals (describe)
  - people with disabilities similar to those of the person they care for
  - any people applying for these same kind of benefits

- Information about benefits; including using different media
  - complexity of benefits

- If improvements were made:
  - how should they be communicated (eg target versus general broadcast)

12. <u>Awareness/Experience of Special Facilities for Sick/People with disabilities</u>

- Have they heard of any special facilities for people with disabilities; eg wider doors, ramps; staff who can sign, staff visits to groups; tapes, etc. (what)
  - experience of using them
  - views about use

- Experience of the person they care for using special facilities; satisfaction

- What special facilities would they like to see available for people with disabilities similar to the that of the person they care for

- What would empower people with this type of disability to be more independent (in accessing and claiming benefits)

13. <u>The recipients' views (Ask only where interviewing both claimant and carer)</u>

- Nature of Sickness/Disability (briefly)
  - nature of sickness/disability
  - how long have they had it
  - has it changed over time (how)

- Effects of Sickness/Disability
  PROBE: mobility; reading; communication; handling money; ability to work

- Perceptions of sickness/disability
  - how do they see themselves; sick?; disabled; etc
  - would they read a leaflet that was marked for people who were 'sick' or 'disabled'

- Reasons for not making own benefit claims
  - would they know how to

- Feelings about help with making claims
  - control over money
  - trust
  - privacy
  - independence

- What would empower them to be more independent (in accessing and claiming benefits)?

  eg. physical access; better advice; changed claim forms; home visits; different sort of assistance; information on different media

P5173 TG4/4 Stage 1

Benefit information needs of people with long term sickness or disability

TOPIC GUIDE FOR VOLUNTARY & STATUTORY AGENCIES

Throughout the interview emphases should be placed on:

a) the effect of different disabilities on gaining access to the benefit system;

b) the effect of that experience on making subsequent/future claims;

c) potential solutions that will empower people with disabilities to make their own claims.

1. Background

- Name of organisation
- Role in organisation; how long in that role
- Brief summary of organisation's work
- Contact with long term sick/disabled

2. Services Offered (in general & specifically for sick/disabled)

- Services offered by their organisation (general)
- Does their service adequately cover all groups within their remit; why/why not; who is left out
- Special services for long term sick/disabled
  - what are they
  - who are they aimed at; do they target particular groups; do they leave out particular groups
  - why did they decide on this sort of initiative
  - how long has it been in place
  - success of special services; how is success judged
  - methods for obtaining feedback from users
  - plans for future; expansion; continuation; discontinuation; why

3. Dissemination of Information

- Quality of DSS communication (general level)
  - leaflets
    - i) physical accessibility;
    - ii) labelling; identification with labels
    - iii) presentation (formality; user friendly; typeface)
    - iv) complexity of language
    - v) availability in different languages
    - vi) presentation of eligibility requirements (over simplified?)
    - vii) presentation of claims process
    - viii) frequency of updating
    - ix) issues same for all benefits; why/why not
    - x) other issues of importance

  - Freeline / BEL

    - i) accessibility; can people get through; have people heard of it
    - ii) quality of information; accurate; updated specific to case; comprehensible
    - iii) quantity of information; related only to specific questions or general advice
    - iv) quality of service same for all benefits; why/why not
    - v) would they recommend using the Advice Line; why/why not
    - vi) other issues of importance

- Claim Forms

    i) accessibility; easy to get; do people know where to go
    ii) presentation; formality; user friendly; typeface (style & size)
    iii) complexity of language; clarity of instructions; problems for non English speakers or English as second language
    iv) different forms; experiences; preferences
    v) presentation of supporting evidence required; clear; detailed
    vi) problems for particular groups
    vii) other problems

- Quality of relationship between DSS/BA & Clients

    i) do clients trust DSS/BA information; why/why not
    ii) atmosphere at DSS/BA; helpfulness; physical environment & accessibility; labelling
    iii) would a client's first choice for information be the DSS/BA; why/why not
    iv) is there somewhere else that would be a better source of information; where; why
        - would you recommend the other source before the DSS/BA; why/why not

- Quality of Other Sources of Information
    - What other sources of benefits information are available (especially for people with long term sickness/disabilities)
    i) voluntary organisations; which
        - do they give personal advice
        - do they deal with all types of sickness/disability benefit
        - are they better with some than others; which
        - do they help with claims & appeals
        - would they recommend them; why/why not
        - are these the right organisations to be helping with enquiries/claims; why/why not; who should help

    ii) statutory organisations; which
        - do they give personal advice
        - do they deal with all types of sickness/disability benefit
        - are they better with some than others; which
        - do they help with claims & appeals
        - would they recommend them; why/why not
        - are these the right organisations to be helping with enquiries/claims; why/why not; who should help

- Local Problems with Dissemination of Information

    - particular problems in their area; what are they
    i) Accessibility (rural, geographically dispersed, public transport, etc...)
    ii) Physical access
    iii) Availability (presence of local offices; hours of offices; staffing of offices, etc)
    iv) Expertise (training in benefits, especially sickness/disability; awareness of changes to benefits, etc)
    v) contacting target groups; any groups not covered/especially hard to reach
    vi) presence of support services (someone to help with actual claim/appeals, etc)
    vii) other problems

4. <u>Awareness of Change- DSS/Benefits Agency (briefly)</u>

- Knowledge of Changes in the DSS
    - the Benefits Agency
    - feelings about changes
    i) perceived need for change
    ii) is this the change that was needed; why/why not

- perceived impact of change locally
- satisfaction with communication about changes

- Knowledge of new benefits; DWA/DLA
  - feelings about changes
    - i) perceived need for change
    - ii) is this the change that was needed; why/why not
  - perceived impact of change locally
  - satisfaction with communication about changes

- Suggestions
  - how changes should be communicated

5. Improvements Needed

- Suggestions for how DSS could improve services for sick/disabled especially
  - leaflets
  - Benefits Advice Line
  - claim forms
  - offices (physical environment, etc...)
  - staffing
  - media used to advertise benefits
  - types of media campaigns; broadcast or targetted; why

- How should improvements be funded

- If extra resources available how should this money be spent; by whom

- Suggestions for how services for sick/disabled could be improved locally
  - accessibility
  - availability
  - expertise
  - contacting clients; targeting specific groups; who; why/why not;
  - provision of support services
  - others
  - problems preventing the suggested changes
    - i) what are they
    - ii) why
    - iii) how could they be addressed

Benefit information needs of people
with long term sickness or disability

The guide shows which of the target groups each set of topics most applies to. Groups listed in square brackets are marginal for that topic:

Car *Claimants*
Car *Carers*
Adv *Advisors*

1. **Experience of making a claim for benefit**
(To be covered briefly and used as context for the 'solutions' part of the interview)

- Awareness of benefits
  - how did they find out; sources of information
  - when did they find out

- Determining eligibility
  - why did they think they were eligible; any hesitations

- Making a claim
  - how did they decide to make a claim
  - any sources of advice or help; what; why needed
  - reasons for delayed claim
  - *failed claims* (if any); what failed; understanding of why claim failed
  - *changed claims* (if any); what changed; understanding of what changed

- Seeking advice
  - any help or advice sought; what was it; why sought
  - did they know what to ask
  - did/do they need any further advice

- Leaflets and forms
  - availability
  - ease of use
  - effect of experience on subsequent claims
  - use of other media (tapes, etc); need for

- Medical assessments
  - experiences and views (if relevant)
  - effect of experience on subsequent claims

- Communicating with the DSS/BA
  - how do they get in touch with DSS/BA
  - under what circumstances
  - experiences and views

2. **Identification with descriptions/labels** **Cla Car Adv**
Explore the meanings and resonances of different terms to describe people with disabilities

a. How do they think of/describe themselves? What would they like to be called, identified as?
b. How do they react to terms like 'sick & disabled'? Do they see leaflet FB28 (or FB31 for carers) as 'for them or not for them', because it is labelled 'Sick & disabled'?
c. How do they picture people who are 'sick'? And how do they picture 'disabled'? What do they think is the public image of these terms?
d. How do they react or relate to terms like 'ill', 'unwell', 'handicapped' etc. How do they feel about being described in these terms?

e. How do they react to words like 'carer' or 'helper' (where applicable)?
f. How do they react to the words, phrases, descriptions listed on prompt cards - and others which may emerge in conversation? (Show or read from prompt cards B - H)
g. Ask carers how they perceive themselves, and how they perceive those they care for.
h. Ask claimants how they perceive their carers as well as themselves
i. Do carers who are family/friends of claimant think of themselves as playing a specific role - and how do they describe it?
j. How does all the above affect claiming behaviour, perceived eligibility?
k. Is there a problem with degrees of sickness/disability - how severe does problem have to be to claim? Does this affect claiming?

3. Benefit enquiry line (BEL) **Cla Ca Adv**

a. Are they aware of BEL?
b. What do they think it does, how it works, what it can do for them?
c. Do they distinguish it from Freeline? Do they know about that, and have they used it?
d. Have they had experience of using BEL? What for? With what result? How useful? How satisfactory?
e. Does it sound useful or not? Why?
f. ***Show descriptive sheet or BEL leaflet.*** Make it clear that it covers all benefits but specialises in disability benefits.
g. How does this match with expectations? How does it sound now? Would it solve any of their problems? Would it have been useful to them in the past?
h. When and how might they use BEL? How likely?
i. Perceived advantages and disadvantages?
j. What changes would be necessary to make BEL really useful?

4. Videotape **Cla Adv Ca**

Show all or part of the DWA/DLA video to some of the claimants groups. (We are interested in the properties and usefulness of the medium for explaining benefits to the target group, rather than an evaluation of this particular tape. If this tape has problems or disadvantages explore what could to be done to get round them)

a. Do they have video replay facilities?
b. Do they recall seeing DLA/DWA adverts? If so, how did they react to it at the time? Where did they see it (BBC? ITV/Ch4? At a meeting? etc)
c. Do they find it informative/uninformative? Interesting/dull? Easy/hard to follow?
d. How does it compare with reading a leaflet as a way of finding out about disability benefits? Or with other information sources?
e. If more of these were issued covering other disability benefits would they find it helpful or not? And in what ways?
f. What sort of information is videotape particularly good for?

Participants can be asked generally about the uses of videotape even where this is not actually played in the session.

5. Audiotape **Cla (especially visually impaired) [Adv? Ca?]**

Play all or some of one of the available audiotapes in selected sessions. Objectives and line of questioning as for videotape.

6. Materials for people with visual impairment **Cla (blind, partially sighted, elderly) Adv**

a. In interviews with partially sighted and blind explore how they normally cope with written material from any source. Also what is the role and potential of braille - how far used, advantages and disadvantages.
b. In interviews with the elderly and partially sighted explore the use of materials printed in larger type. Use the DWA/DLA claim packs to explore this.
    i. How useful? To whom? Whether seen examples?
    ii. How large does the typeface need to be?
    iii. Does larger typeface increase legibility/motivation even for those who are not visually impaired?

7. Carer leaflet **Car Adv [Cla]**

Show a copy

a. Have they seen it? Have they got a copy? Have they read it?
b. Would they pick it up?
c. Do they identify with the term carer? With the question on the cover? Explore ways of referring to carers using prompt card I.
d. Reactions to Carer leaflet?
e. Does it seem useful? Understandable? Informative? Does it tell them anything they don't know? (leave copy?)
f. Reactions to organisations list in Carers leaflet

8. DLA/DWA **Cla Adv [Car?]**

We do not need to evaluate DWA, DLA materials as such - other research has done that. But are there any lessons that can be learnt from this recent introduction for communications and access to S & D benefits in general?

a. How far are people now aware of the change to these benefits from AA and MobA? Do they now understand what is available and how it works?
b. Awareness of publicity campaign
c. Reactions to publicity: Literature? TV? Claim packs?
d. Reactions to concept/practice of medical self-assessment
e. For anyone who has made a claim for DWA/DLA, how well did this go? What problems? Any problems with forms, claim packs?
f. Did they see any of the TV programmes about DWA/DLA? On which channel?

9. Liaison officers **(Adv Cla Car)**

Some Benefits Agency offices have specialist Benefits Advisors (covering the full range of benefits). All have District Information Officers who visit and speak to local groups etc. These are separate from Visiting Officers, who visit claimants with mobility problems in their homes.

a. How useful would it be to have:
   - a designated source of **special expertise in disability benefits** within the local office?
   - more activity in visiting, speaking to and distributing literature to relevant groups and organisations within the community?
b. Are these things already seen to happen? With what effect?
c. Have people been to any talks/visits? What impressions?
d. What kinds of group should be visited, and to do what?

10. Sources of information/advice/help **[Cla Car [Adv]**

Probe further on whether/where claimants and carers get information, advice or help:

a. **When** do they go for information, help, advice?
b. **Who** do they turn to for:
   information?
   advice?
   help?
c. How satisfactory? What problems, lacks, limitations, gaps?
d. How useful do they find different sources?
e. How do they perceive DSS/BA as a sources?
f. Awareness of existing organisations (local and national)
g. Use/membership of organisations? For what?
h. How far do people use phone services (eg DIAL, BEL, DSS Freeline)? How useful? What could make them more useful? Attitudes to using the telephone/ Problems (eg speech impairment)

11. Advisors' needs **Adv**

a. What kinds of information do they need about benefits for people with disabilities?
b. What are their current sources? What do they use most? What used in what situations?
c. What is the role of publications like:
   Disability Rights Handbook?
   Other voluntary sectory publications?
   DSS claimant literature (Show FB 28, FB 31)
   DSS technical literature
   Other sources?
d. How adequate are these sources? What are the gaps or weaknesses in provision? What other needs exist?
e. What is the information providing role of DSS *vis a vis* agencies?
   What sorts of information need to come (or come best) **from DSS?**
   What sorts of information do the **voluntary sector** provide best? And why?
f. What are the pros and cons of DSS providing information?
g. How far do DSS need to encourage or sponsor voluntary sector provision, and why?
h. (In Berkshire) How is the Berkshire pilot of the DoH National Disability Information Project going? What effects on:
   Information provision?
   Access to S&D benefits?
i. How far have they used video (DSS or other)? For what purposes? What potential and for what?

12. LOAF and BAP **Adv**

These are three compact information systems provided for local office staff.

a. Do agencies know about them? Have any got copies?
b. These are not currently supposed to be available outside the Benefits Agency - but if they were made available to agencies, as a system with updates:
   i. How helpful would they be?
   ii. Would they help improve access to disability benefits?
   iii. What kinds of agency would find them most helpful?
   iv. What role would they play? How would they be used?
   v. How would they compare with (eg) the Disability Rights Handbook?
   vi. Are they sufficiently detailed?
c. How well done are they seen to be?
   - Format (which preferred)?
   - Layout?
   - Language?
   - Ease/speed of access?
   - Comprehensiveness?
   - Detail?

13. Benefit wheel **Adv [Cla? Car?]**

Show the RCN benefits wheel, to see whether a similar device targeted specifically at benefits for the sick & disabled would be useful. It might work along the lines of the LOAF index cards, listing people's situations round the circumference, and possible benefits down the slot.

a. See if anyone can think of a different way of achieving the same effect - ie an easy reference item?
b. What about people with visual impairment or manipulation problems?

14. Computer routines **Adv**

Demonstrate the Jarman or Ferret programme as briefly as possible to advisors, starting to work through a sample case, and then showing prepared printout.

a. Do they know about this or similar software? Do any have experience of it? Do any have a copy? What is their experience? How useful? For what? What problems? How could it be improved?

b. How many have relevant hardware? PC or other systems? Could they use it if they had it?
c. How useful does it look? In general? For disabled claimants? Would it help improve access to disability benefits?
d. Strengths? Weaknesses? Problems? Opportunities?

15. Flow chart — Adv

We do not have any worked-up examples of a 'flow-chart' approach to signposting benefits worth applying for, but the general concept could be explored with advisors, in the context of looking at computer routines, BAP/LOAF and the benefits wheel.

a. If a suitable flow chart could be devised, how useful would it be:
   i) to advisors?
   ii) to customers?

Card A

Severe Disablement Allowance

Invalidity Benefit

Invalid Care Allowance

Disability Living Allowance (DLA)

Disability Working Allowance (DWA)

Attendance allowance

Mobility allowance

Industrial Injuries Disablement Benefit

Income Support: **with Special Needs Premium**
Income Support: **without Special Needs Premium**

Unemployment Benefit

Social Fund

Housing Benefit

Community Charge Benefit

Card B

Sick

Ill

Unwell

Invalid

Unhealthy

Suffering with health problems

Card C

Disabled

Incapacitated

Handicapped

Impaired

Handicap

Visually impaired

Hearing impaired

Card D

Mental health problem

Mental illness

Psychiatric problem

Nervous problem

Depression

Anxiety

Stress problems

Problem with nerves

Card E

Mental handicap

Learning difficulties

Learning disabilities

Mental disabilities

Card F

Do you have any kind of physical or mental condition which makes it hard (or impossible) for you to:

- get a job?
- look after yourself?
- get about?
- live a normal life?

Card G

Do you have any kind of illness, disability or handicap?

Do you have any kind of health problem?
Temporary or permanent? Physical or mental?

Card H

I have a disability

I am disabled

Card I

Carer

Helper

Minder

Someone who gives assistance to ...

Someone who helps ...

Someone who looks after ...

Someone who helps to look after ...

Someone who takes responsibility for ...

Someone who looks after, cares for, or helps ...

Other Research Reports available:

No.	Title	ISBN	Price
1.	Thirty Families: Their Living Standards in Unemployment	0 11 761683 4	£6.65
2.	Disability. Household Income & Expenditure	0 11 761755 5	£5.65
3.	Housing Benefit Review	0 11 761821 7	£16.50
4.	Social Security & Community Care: The Case of Invalid Care Allowance	0 11 761820 9	£9.70
5.	The Attendance Allowance Medical Examination: Monitoring Consumer Views	0 11 761819 5	£5.50
6.	Lone Parent Families in the UK	0 11 761868 3	£11.95
7.	Incomes In and Out of Work	0 11 761910 8	£17.20
8.	Working the Social Fund	0 11 761952 3	£9.00
9.	Evaluating the Social Fund	0 11 761953 1	£22.00
10.	Benefits Agency National Customer Survey 1991	0 11 761956 6	£16.00
11.	Customer Perceptions of Resettlement Units	0 11 761976 0	£13.75
12.	Survey of Admissions to London Resettlement Units	0 11 761977 9	£8.00
13.	Researching the Disability Working Allowance Self Assessment Form	0 11 761834 9	£7.25
14.	Child Support Unit National Client Survey 1992	0 11 762060 2	£30.00
15.	Implementation of Council Tax Benefit	0 11 762061 0	£5.65
16.	Contributions Agency Customer Satisfaction Survey 1992	0 11 762064 5	£18.00
17.	Employers' Choice of Pension Schemes: Report of a Qualitative Study	0 11 762073 4	£5.00
18.	GPs and IVB: A Qualitative Study of the Role of GPs in the Award of Invalidity Benefit	0 11 762077 7	£12.00
19.	Invalidity Benefit: A Survey of Recipients	0 11 762087 4	£10.75
20.	Invalidity Benefit: A Longitudinal Survey of New Recipients	0 11 762088 2	£19.95
21.	Support for Children: A Comparison of Arrangements in Fifteen Countries	0 11 762089 0	£22.95
22.	Pension Choices: A Survey on Personal Pensions in Comparison with Other Pension Options	0 11 762091 2	£18.95
23.	Crossing National Frontiers: An Examination of the Arrangements for Exporting Social Security Benefits in 12 OECD Countries	0 11 762101 3	£17.75
25.	Lone Parents and Work	0 11 762148 x	£12.95
26.	The Effects of Benefit on Housing Decisions	0 11 762157 9	£18.50
	Social Security Research Yearbook 1990–91	0 11 761747 4	£8.00
	Social Security Research Yearbook 1991–92	0 11 761833 0	£12.00
	Social Security Research Yearbook 1992–93	0 11 762150 1	£13.75

Further information regarding other publications available in the Department of Social Security's research series may be obtained from:

Department of Social Security
Attn. Keith Watson
Social Research Branch
Analytical Services Division 5
10th Floor, Adelphi
1–11 John Adam Street
London WC2N 6HT

Telephone: 071 962 8557

Printed in the United Kingdom for HMSO.
Dd.0297745, 5/94, C7, 3396/4, 5673, 277336.